SOME SONGS AND POEMS FROM
RABINDRANATH TAGORE

Some Songs and Poems
from
Rabindranath Tagore

Translated by
PRATIMA BOWES

EAST WEST PUBLICATIONS
LONDON AND THE HAGUE

First published in Great Britain in 1984 by

East-West Publications (UK) Ltd
Jubilee House, Chapel Road, Hounslow, Middlesex, TW3 1XT
Reprinted 1985

Typeset in 10pt Baskerville, By Gilbert Composing Services,
Leighton Buzzard, Bedfordshire, England.

Printed and bound in Great Britain by
Whitstable Litho Ltd., Kent.

Tagore, Rabindranath
    Some songs and poems from Rabindranath Tagore
    I. Title
    891'.4415   PR6039.A2

    ISBN 0-85692-055-X

To
Nita and Alf

Acknowledgements

I am grateful to my daughter, Mrs Nita Clarke, for some of her suggestions for improvement of these translations, and to my friend and former colleague, Mrs Amita Chakravorty of Shri Shikshayatan College, Calcutta, who kindly helped me with the notes. I am obliged to the Visva-Bharati authorities for their kind permission for the publication of this translation.

Contents

SONGS
(first line)

POEMS

Publication date of volumes included in this Selection

Manasi	1890
Sonay Tari	1893-91
Chitra	1895-96
Kshanika	1900-01
Kheya	1906
Utsarga	1914
Balaka	1916
Purabi	1925-26
Parisesh	1932-33
Punasca	1932-33
Bithika	1935-36
Sesh Saptak	1935-36
Patraput	1936-37
Shyamali	1936-37
Prantik	1937-38
Sejuti	1940-41
Nabajatak	1940-41
Sanai	1940-41
Rogsajyay	1940
Arogya	1941
Tanmadine	1941
Seshlekha	1941

Songs were written individually over a long period of Tagore's life and they are published in a collected volume called *Gitabitan*.

Introduction

Rabindranath Tagore was born in Calcutta on 7 May 1861 in a rich, aristocratic and illustrious family, his grandfather being Prince Dwarkanath Tagore, called prince because of his wealth and liberality, and his father *Maharshi* Debendranath Tagore, called maharshi because of his saintly and sage-like character. The family was rich but Rabindranath was not brought up in the lap of luxury. However, it was a very cultivated and cultured environment where music, poetry, drama and other arts were highly respected and actively pursued by many members of the large Tagore family.

For his education the schools proved disappointing, but gaps in conventional education were more than made up by private tuition in literature – Sanskrit, Bengali, English – music and other branches of knowledge. Also there was the religious temperament and strivings of his father to draw on. Rabindranath's sensitive and versatile genius was directed by these influences to a fruition that is rare, especially in India which had gone through centuries of darkness and sterility in the creative field, apart from political dependence.

These influences would not have produced anything so spectacular had it not been for the abundance of his own innate life-force which overflew in many directions. He was a pathfinder in educational policy, an ardent experimenter in agriculture, cooperative societies and rural development, a patriot and at the same time an internationalist who spoke out at every critical juncture in his country's and world's affairs, a painter of a distinctive style that speaks a language entirely different from his poetry ("primitive" painting), and a musical innovator to boot, who not only wrote over two thousand songs but gave them a special kind of melodic structure with his name stamped on it. All these over and above his staggering literary production; staggering in scope, quantity and quality. Among his creations are 12 novels, 11 verse or musical dramas, three dance dramas, four satire and farce, several volumes of short stories, a number of travel diaries, essays on diverse topics like literature, language, history, religion, philosophy, education, essays on great men like Gandhi and

Rammohun Roy, 44 volumes of poetry (several of which are prose poetry, some are in the language of everyday speech, some written in nursery rhyme style, some doggerels, some are narratives in verse, some about children), one book on popular science, and a book of reminiscences on his own life. As for quality, some of his productions in every genre, including novels, are among the best in the Bengali language which itself was largely fashioned by him.

Rabindranath's literary activity started early and it continued to the very end, 1941, when he was eighty years old and very ill. He wrote his first verse at the age of eight and his first narrative poem was published when he was fourteen. Even before his first visit to England at seventeen began his serious literary activity in poetry, novel, drama, song, and narratives. This was the time when he got recognition (but under an assumed name, Bhanusingha) by writing a distinctive style of love poetry, called *Padavali*, after the style of medieval Vaishnava poets, the subject of which is love of Radha and Krishna. Such was his success in recreating this distinctive style that it was taken seriously by some to be the work of the medieval poet Bhanusingha himself.

After his return from England in 1880 he produced his first drama in music, an entirely new thing in Bengali, both in style of music and literary conception. His first book of verse to be included in any collection is *Sandhya Sangeet* (Evening Song, 1881–82) and although it is unmistakably poetry and Tagorean at that, it is also unmistakably adolescent in its effusion of feeling and imagination, and in its boundless sorrow and anguish. This is followed by another volume, *Prabhat Sangeet* (Morning Song, 1883-84, in-between he wrote his first novel) which is the opposite of *Evening Song* in mood. In his reminiscences Tagore says that he had had, before the writing of this book, a mystical experience in which everything was seen as bathed in joy and this poetry gives ample evidence of his new-found joy of existence. But *Prabhat Sangeet* too lacks restraint and the joy appears excessive. The first important drama in verse *Prakritir Pratisodh* was written in 1883, followed by another book of poems *Chabi O Gan* (Pictures and Songs).

In December 1883 he got married.

According to the poet himself it is in his next book of poems *Kari O Komal* (Sharps and Flats, 1886-87) that he has turned his attention from his own inner feelings to the world outside. This is not quite accurate though. In his previous two volumes the outside world has its share and in *Kari O Komal* alongside his deep acceptance of life and his love of this world one can find a strain of sadness which is controlled compared to the effusiveness of *Sandhya Sangeet*, but is sadness nonetheless. This is not unexpected as this volume was written after the loss of his very dear sister-in-law who had played a large part in his life. Between 1886 and 1890 were written *Rajarshi*, a novel; *Mayar Khela*, (Of the Mind).

Manashi shows many characteristics that are typically Tagorean, his exquisite and abiding sense of lyrical beauty, love of nature in all its moods, interest in social, political, national and 'mystical' aspects of man's existence. The poet has now matured into an artist both in theme and technique and has learned restraint and control in the use of language. And there is also a deep awareness that nature and creation can and do frustrate man's deepest longings, and plunge him into the darkest despair. Contrary to the popular image of Tagore as an one-eyed man who saw only light and love this understanding of and sympathy with misery and despair are also typically Tagorean.

The Tagore family had a large estate in a village in East Bengal (now Bangladesh) and he had observed the peasants and their sorrowful and meagre existence at close quarters. He had even tried to improve their lot through various schemes while managing the estate from a boat on the river Padma. This intimate association with nature and man provided him with some of the beautiful imagery for his poetry. The experience of misery and sorrow neither turned him into a nihilist nor made him declare that life is absurd and God is dead. Occasionally it brought him on the verge of it though, and later on I shall say something on how he coped with his day-light awareness of human misery. Here I only want to make the point that Tagore was fully aware of both good and evil and this makes him the man of amazing breadth of vision that he was, supplying the necessary tension out of which all great art is created.

Tagore was well acquainted with the rich store of myths and legends that Hindu (and Buddhist) culture possesses and some of his creations are reworking of these in his characteristic fashion which transformed a simple story into a drama of psychological tension, often possessing symbolic and spiritual significance beyond its literal meaning. In 1891 he wrote *Chitrangada*, a musical drama, based on a story in the *Mahabharata* and in the same year was produced a social comedy, *Goray Galad*, sparkling with wit and satire. Between 1894 and 1900 he produced seven major volumes of verse, besides drama, short stories, and other prose writings. This was just before his distinctively religious period which starts with *Naivedya* (1901) when he produced the books that go into the making of the *Gitanjali*. To this pre-religious period belong *Sonar Tari, Chitra, Chaitali, Kalpana, Kshanika, Katha,* and *Kahini* (the last two being narrative verses). These are rich and varied both in technique and content. In these books tiredness and dejection is not entirely absent; however it is now tempered by detachment (not non-involvement; he was intimately involved with life at every stage) and reflection. *Kshanika* particularly, produced when the poet was forty years old, is remarkable in its combination of serious thought with ease of expression, lightness of mood and brisk rhythm. It is playful, almost frivolous in tone at times but not in content. The contrast of this poetry with highly ornamental and sonorous verse that Tagore also produced in fair measure is obvious. In *Chitra* Tagore develops the image of what he calls his 'life-deity', not to be confused with God, but, his own inner creative power, something which, he believed, was in control of his life rather than being under his control. Often this idea of 'life-deity' mingles with the image of the beloved and no doubt it is sometimes treated as the Divine itself. But it is a distinct idea and through this idea Tagore paid homage to the creative genius that he found in himself and which, he felt, lived in him as a double, so to say.

In the next period of his life we find him as an educator inaugurating his ideal school at Santiniketan, West Bengal, in a peaceful village setting, which eventually developed into a university. (This village connection both in East and West Bengal provided him with the necessary environment for his experiments in agiculture and rural development.) It is also a period when he wrote several novels, the first of their kind in any of the Indian languages. But it is his personal life that saw a major change during this period, loss of his wife, a daughter and a son in the course of a few years. This loss was deeply felt but instead of making him bitter it developed into a sincere personal longing and love for the divine power in the universe which he believed guides our destiny to some ultimate fulfilment. The result was some devotional and religious poetry, superb in its simplicity and sincerity, some of which in English translation as *Gitanjali* brought him the Nobel prize and worldwide fame.

It was an accident that the translations in prose that Tagore had made of some of his relgious poetry, purely for his own pleasure and as a leisure-time activity, were discovered during hs visit to England in 1912 by some distinguished people. Many, including W.B. Yeats, went rapturous over them possibly because the poetry was something that the western world was no longer producing but deep down had not outgrown the need for, mystical poetry after the fashion of the Old Testament.

In my view, Tagore richly deserved his fame as a great poet and his recognition by the Nobel prize committee. But at the same time, I take it as a misfortune that his fame happened to be based on the English version of the *Gitanjali*. This for several reasons. It created a myth (as myth once created dies hard) that Tagore is a mystical and devotional poet, which is only a fraction of the truth about him. This much should be clear from what I have already said about his literary development and productions. Soon after the Nobel prize in 1913 he hastily translated (published by Macmillan), often in a mutilated version, some of his highly symbolic writings: poetry, drama, and allegorical story. This put the seal on his reputation as a mystic. (The translations were generally bad and later on when the charm of mysticism had worn off in a changed literary climate they were found vague, woolly and meaningless by most western readers.)

To go back to *Gitanjali*. Some people in their encounter with *Gitanjali* thought that it was influenced by the Old Testament and I for one cannot blame them. For the approach there, reminiscent of the intensity and earnestness of the Old Testament, and the style with its 'Thee' and 'Thou' that creates a distance between all-powerful God and creaturely man are distinctly Biblical. The tone of the Bengali *Gitanjali*, on the other hand, is calm and it is quite different in approach. For the most part, it treats God as an intimate and beloved friend who in his turn awaits love from man and who is not quite complete in his majestic aloneness without this exchange. There is about these poems an atmosphere of domestic simplicity, a man to man emotional exchange, which is foreign to what is ordinarily known as mystical or devotional poetry where man offers total self-surrender to an all powerful God. No doubt a few poems in the *Gianjali* do talk of this surrender that is typical of a devotional attitude but most of them read like lover poetry where love of nature and love of man (woman) single and become one with love of God; and God is not in heaven, he is everywhere, in the sights and sounds and colour of this earth, in the autumn sun and the rainy-season flood, and he is certainly in man's heart. The English *Gitanjali* is great devotional or mystical literature but it is not great poetry and no wonder it soon outlived its fame as such. The Bengali *Gitanjali* is excellent religious love poetry, not devotional literature, and as love poetry it has a certain grace, ease and charm of style that is missing in the serious and sombre prose of the English.

Nevertheless I would not call even the Bengali *Gitanjali* the best example of Tagore's creative genius whether in scope of feeling – the *Gitanjali's* concern, as noted by many, is the poet's purely personal relationship with God – or skill in execution of ideas that one can find in his later poetry where even the issue of man's understanding of God acquires a new depth because it is now aware of all that stands in the way of an easy faith. The avid acceptance of the *Gitanjali* in the West perhaps made Tagore feel, even if subconsciously, that anything smacking of mysticism would go down well with western readers – the reason why he picked the pieces he did for translation out of his considerable literary output. It also explains the manner in which he did it. The result is that when literary fashion changed after the holocaust of the First World War and critics came to demand stark realism of the most naked sort rather than romantic and idealistic attitudes that saw the world as basically good, even Yeats, who had at one point thought that the *Gitanjali* contained the type of poetry he would have liked to have written himself, denounced Tagore's writings as sugary literature that is completely out of touch. Had Tagore's fame not been built on the *Gitanjali* his standing as a great poet and literary figure, comparable to other great figures, could not have been eclipsed by the thirties, as it was to all intents and purposes.

However, to take the story up. After the *Gitanjali* period came *Balaka* (1916) with its new kind of rhythm to suit the new mood (post-First World War). The poetry of *Balaka* speaks of movement that is inherent in all creation and the need to leave behind all that is dead and sterile in one's search for significance. Along with this matures his conception of God. The image is no longer of a loving and dear friend waiting to offer security and fulfilment after heartbreak. He is now also 'the terrible' who demands utmost sacrifice from man. The Puranic deity, Rudra the auspicious-terrible, who destroys as much as he creates now becomes the symbol of the divine. This deity offers no consolation; he leaves man to fight his own battle, and indeed his love often comes in the guise of cruelty in the face of which all that man can do is to learn to accept it in detachment. It is true that with detachment peace comes in the end, even a vision of the terrible as beautiful, but all this is dearly bought by man's own effort, not freely offered by a loving God. Tagore does not, of course, abandon the idea of a deep bond of love that exists between man and the ultimate reality that exists beyond all human reckoning of good and evil. But this love can only be felt in aesthetic detachment and Tagore has to use the old Puranic idea of God's play *(lila)* to reconcile himself to what, on purely human terms, appears as 'unacceptable cruelty'. Often the reconciliation achieved breaks down and the question 'why?' raises its head all over again, especially in the poetry of his last ten years. The tension continues and it expresses itself in restless search and some magnificent poetry. This search did not quite recover the earlier easy faith of the *Gitanjali* period where there was an implicit assurance of ultimate good coming out of all this suffering. But it does not quite end in disbelief either. What it finally succeeds in achieving, except in moments of breakdown, is a mature detachment that is able to take it all by seeing everything as part of a totality wherein all things have their justification (aesthetic and not moral) simply because they are there, no matter whether they serve the purpose of man's happiness or not. Indeed to achieve this detachment man must cease to demand happiness of God. Looked at in this way even the terrible achieves a kind of aesthetic beauty and what man should do is to learn to see this sublime beauty in the terrible (sublime, because it ranges far beyond man's concern for happiness, taking everything in its sweep that man for his purposes calls 'good', 'bad' or 'indifferent'). Reacting by despair and rejection is no way to live, and hope of divine help is simply self-deception.

This understanding progressively deepens after *Balaka*, but the heart-break is never finally over. Tagore continues to say both that all futility can be transformed by man into a sublime joy and this is what life is all about, and that it is hard to find any sense in all the agony and despair that are heaped on helpless man. Meanwhile he continues to create as before, novels, poems, prose reflections, travelogues, satire, plays, more poems and so it goes on. At seventy he produces some beautiful love lyrics and starts a new activity, a style of painting that is new in India. And between seventy and eighty he concentrates more or less on prose poetry of a complex and sophisticated kind, yet another innovation of technique. Amongst these latest volumes are *Parisesh, Punasca, Shyamali, Sesh Saptak, Sejuti, Patraput, Nabajatak, Rogsajyay, Arogya* and *Sesklekha.* In these books creative tension continues over all manner of problems, even his own being. Tagore was full of wonder about hs own creative genius, which was a mystery and a most intimate reality, and this he held in the highest respect. And yet there were times when he felt inadequate and unfulfilled in being just a poet (which is not factually true). At times he found fulfilment through a deep sense of unity with all existence; and at other times his sense of loneliness as an individual took over. Sometimes he thought that finding beauty in the terrible would give significance to all of life; at other times he felt that it is only some 'immortal' moments when the infinite breaks into the finite that give significance to man's life; to ask for more is futile. In his last book of poems, *Seshlekha* (Last Writings), he asks the most fundamental question of all: Who Am I? The last poem in this collection where the sun asks the newly emerged existence, 'who are you?' shows Tagore's quest for an answer. But Tagore would not have been the great poet that he was if he ever knew, once for all, and in this last poem written towards the end of his life no answer was found. He had to continually reopen all questions as life moved on the new experiences crowded on him. Still, he continued to love this world and life, such as it is; continued to find beauty in man, nature and even in the terrible God who offers no help but in finding whom man transcends suffering. I agree with those who find that the description that fits him most is not of a 'mystic' but of a 'lover'.

According to some critics it is in his last ten years that he produced his best when not only his thought but his language has acquired a rare degree of economy, control, precision and sharpness, along with breadth of sympathy and vision. But inevitably prose poetry cannot but lose lyrical character and this makes others declare that the poetry of this period is just prose refashioned and his best is to be found in the period of the lyrics, in *Manashi, Chitra, Balaka, Purabi,* and the like. Naturally this is a question of taste and what I have tried here is to include something from most periods (except the effusive poetry of the very early period) so that a more or less balanced picture is available.

Unfortunately my choice had to be severely limited by translatability. For had I always chosen pieces that, in Bengali, showed his best (both in quality and variety) but which I was unable to translate poetically, I would have done a great disservice to Tagore who had already suffered greatly, in comparison with any other great literary figure from bad translation. Tagore's feeling for language, sense of rhythm and the rich suggestibility of the metaphors he used (metaphors create one of the greatest problems of translation, for associations that exist in one language do not exist in another) made the task all the more challenging. I have endeavoured to keep these translations close to Tagore in every way: ideas, structure of sentences, rhythm, even his turn of phrases where possible, except for adding or deleting (but very rarely) a word or two here and there, for the sake of rhythm or rhyme. These are as literal as any translation can be. For translations exist which try more to convey the grandeur of his thought (much in the manner of the *Gitanjali*) than his poetry, but thought alone did not make Tagore the artist he was. Tagore's own translations, hastily done, are, generally speaking, poor. At least they do nothing to exhibit the beauty or the poetic quality of their Bengali originals. And even if good translations, done by others, of some poems do already exist, I think that in the case of a great poet like Tagore several versions of the same poem can and should exist in translation, considering that translation in another language rarely does justice to the original. Whether my translations are good, both as translation and in their own right as poetry, it is for others to say, but as a collection it at least brings into one compass a representative selection of the richness and variety one can find in Tagore of all periods; and not many such selections exist. Translation of the poetry that belongs to the post-*Gitanjali* period is particularly needed to counter the myth of mysticism and devotionalism. Anyway, selections like mine are important to re-establish Tagore in his rightful place as a poet of world stature, someone whose poetry will stand the test of time because it is truly universal, however much it draws on the sights and sounds of Bengal and myths and legends of the Hindu and Buddhist cultures.

This is not to say that some of the symbolism and sentiments in Tagore may not appear strange or unfamiliar to western readers. Tagore was steeped in the Upanisads, even if he interpreted them in a non-traditional way. This gives a certain cosmic dimension to some of his poetry. The Upanisads offer a world-view that is very different from the religion of monotheism which lies at the basis of western culture. However, their very strangeness may appear to be an attraction, now, unlike in the period of western cultural insularity betwen the two world wars when Tagore's fame quickly eclipsed because of what was thought to be his vague 'upanisadism', if I may coin such a word. In the world of 1982 the cultural traffic is no longer one way, from the west to the east. The Upanisads are not only much more known now, they are widely appreciated and the connection of Tagore's poetry with this philosophy may well lead some people to enjoy it rather than be repelled.

I said earlier that till the very end Tagore did not have a final answer as to what it is all about, and who he was. Nevertheless, he did believe most of the time, as he said in his *Atmaparicaya* (Introducing Oneself), that his stance to the world was that of the Upanisads. Perhaps a few words about the Upanisads and what they meant to Tagore may help to understand him better. It will at least make it clear that looking at the world from an Upadisadic point of view need make no one love this world any the less, nor make one sugary or one-eyed. It is, of course, true that there is a very influential religious tradition in India which says that this visible world is an illusion and that this 'truth' has been proclaimed by the Upanisads. Tagore vigorously rejects this interpretation and, in my opinion, rightly so. The idea that God is all good and that his creation was for the purpose of conferring happiness on man is definitely not Upanisadic – the Upanisads posit an ultimate beyond such distinctions as good and evil – neither is it Hindu. It may be a belief that was fostered by the reformed Church of his father, and the reform was done under Christian influence. Tagore eventually abandoned this Church for he found it impossible to believe anything that did not take shape under the light of his own experience. If he believed in the Upanisads he did so in his own way, under his own heart's demands, making it perfectly clear, both in his prose and poetry, that the traditional interpretation, known as *mayavada* (the doctrine of illusion) was for him totally unacceptable.

The Upanisads conceive reality at its ultimate level as *Brahman* (a term in neuter gender) meaning the Divine Immensity (absolute, infinite and of the nature of pure consciousness) which includes all that there is and this reality is not here personalized as a God who stands over against His creation as something distinct from His own reality. It is mythically pictured that in the beginning Brahman was alone but did not like it, so he/it diversified himself/itself into all things of his creation including man, so as to be able to enjoy himself/itself as many. All things are therefore manifestations of Brahman in different name and shape and are non-dual *(advaita)* with it, for all reality is one and there is nothing which is not this reality. The Upanisads urge man to discover himself as *Atman* (Self) which is of the nature of pure consciousness, being, and bliss, for he can then identify himself with Brahman. But this does not mean that only Atmas is Brahman, the rest is not; for it has been said repeatedly that all that is here because Brahman becomes the manifested world, so all this is Brahman (the doctrine of illusion ignores this and says that if Atman is Brahman and there is nothing other than Brahman then only the Self is real; everything else, including this world and man in his particularity, is an illusion). Brahman is characterized as *anand*, the exact meaning of which is conveyed not so much by bliss as by pure delight inherent in Being itself, ranging beyond all distinctions and multiplicities even while embracing it all. Out of this pure delight of Being everything arises, creating the world of distinctions such as good and evil. These distinctions apply in the world of becoming where they are true enough but the truth of this trust, in the language of Upanisads, is Pure Being (so pure delight beyond all thought of happiness or misery), forever enduring even while expressing itself as becoming. And this Pure Being can be realized in man as *Atman* (Self). So man too can find his enduring reality as ranging beyond all distinctions of good and evil, happiness and misery.

The Upanisads clearly consider that everything that there is partakes of the same reality which is both Being and becoming. Of course man's liberation from finitude (and so from suffering) consists in realizing himself as *Atman*, which is to be done by seeing all becoming as grounded in ever-enduring Being. But it is the *seeing of Being in becoming* that interests Tagore; he is not interested in Pure Being in isolation, apart from the world of multiplicity and alone in its majesty. Becoming fascinated him with all its imperfections, contradictions (arising out of conflict of duality, there is no conflict in the One), suffering and evil. But what in his feeling gave this transient reality such inestimable value is its grounding in Being, as the Upanisads say it is grounded. He was in no hurry to bypass the wonder of this manifold world to reach Being beyond all distinctions. What he passionately wanted was rather the touch of this Being – that, from one way of looking at it, lies beyond all distinctions even while expressing itself there – in the very experience of the distinctions themselves, as the living, throbbing presence of Reality forever creating itself as the many of this world out of pure delight. There was, then, no question of renunciation as there is for one who wants Pure Being minus all becoming. But there is need for detachment, the creating of a certain distance in experience through viewing it apart from all question of man's immediate purpose such as attaining happiness or avoiding suffering. Tagore is not advocating the abandonment of such purposes altogether though; becoming and its demands, in their character as becoming, have their place and he did not neglect them just as he did not neglect Being. What he had instead was a daring vision that could see the same reality, simultaneously, from two different points of view. No wonder tension for him was never over as it can be for one who settles for Pure Being to the exclusion of becoming.

Let us now have a look at the *Atmaparicaya* where Tagore develops his own brand of Upanisadic philosophy. I put together below some thoughts from it, more or less following the poet's own words (Bengali), but in an order that is mine:

The world exists through the tension of opposites — life and death, hate and love, selfishness and self-giving. On one side is separation, on the other union, on one side duality and distinction, on the other non-duality, on one side that binds, on the other that, liberates; the finite and the infinite become one by means of the beauty, form and flavour of this world. I am a messenger of this enchanting diversity of existence. To assimilate this play of diversity within myself and then to give it a poetic shape is my job. I am a playmate of the ever-becoming and my task is to carry within me its many flavours. In a poet's composition there are a thousand and one fleeting tunes; but they all indicate the ever-enduring in their different ways. They give pleasure but this pleasure can be had best in detachment. Detachment strengthens, purifies and ennobles our enjoyment of this very world. I know that I have come only to tell this, 'I have looked and loved this world'. I am not a saint, nor a religious practitioner. What I seek is the flavour of delight that has gone into the creation of this universe.

The path of creation is through destruction. If I say 'this is painful' that will be a true statement, but not the last word about creation. I understand life fully when I also say that there is beauty in this pain, and delight too, the delight of the infinite which appears as the terrible to disturb the monotone of our insignificant everydayness. In this tension between the heart of man and the heart of the infinite lies the mystery of creation. We know that time and again the grace and peace of this world are disturbed and man is aggrieved with tension and conflict. As if within the heart of creation resides a 'man one' who tears all things asunder. But I do not want to let go of anything. I am not complete without it all, It is in the nature of truth that all things, even things which appear contradictory, can meet together in its wide expanse. This truth is the deepest basis of the units of all things that exist together in this universe.

There is within me a master who transcends me and who directs my pen. Through great pain and suffering brought by constant parting he is uniting me with that which is beyond all limit. I know that from eternity I have come through many, now forgotten, forms to this, my present expression. That forgotten memory of the immense flow of existence running through this universe, an existence rooted in Him, remains in my unconscious. That is why I feel such a long-standing unity with this world, with trees and plants, birds and beasts; that is why I do not feel that this immense and mysterious universe is terrible, alien or unrelated to me.

Between that which is creating itself within me and the creator there is a relationship of delight, of love. The realization that nothing can exist without this love can bring peace in all our joys and sorrows. He draws to Himself every exuberance of my joy, absorbs within Himself every pain and suffering that I undergo. So I know, nothing that happens to me is in vain. Within the act of creation that flows through eternity my pleasure and pain find their own place.

It is a wonder that I am becoming, I am being expressed. There is within me an infinite grace, that is why I am being nurtured by the power of this boundless universe, among its sun and the moon, its countless stars and planets, that is why I can stand with my eyes open under the sky, amidst its light. What do I offer as a return for this surprising right to existence that has been conferred on me, for the joy and the love that stay in my being, without which I would not be? This colour, this light and shade, this silence of the sky, this wide expanse between the earth and the atmosphere, a constant preparation is going on for all this. We are not even aware that this fantastic event is taking place right before our eyes. From a distance of millions and millions of miles, through thousands of years, light from a star travels to come to us, but this wonder does not touch our heart. For me this world is like a friend of long standing, but like one's beloved it is also ever new.

I have recited the Upanisads from my childhood and my mind has formed the habit of seeing a fullness that transcends but also permeates this world. Love transcends the loved one. Through the beauty of this world, and the grace of the beloved it is He who draws us, nothing else has this power. His love comes through the very love that belongs to this earth and through this embodied love the beauty of what is beyond all form can be seen. To see this is the goal of our spiritual life. It is easy to feel love for nature, for nature offers no obstruction to us. But this is not enough. Love of nature must fulfil itself in the love of humanity and through all this our little 'I' must unite in love with the universal 'I' who is our father, friend, lover, and leader. The poet's work is successful if in his creation the indeterminate and the formless take a body. The world we know through our senses is not the only world. This world is being constantly completed as poets and seers give it an ever-new shape from age to age, through feelings and thoughts that take place in the depth of their hearts. Truth exists in universal form within each man, but each man is also a unique expression of this truth. To express this truth is his religion *(dharma)*. He maintains the fascinating variety of this world through the practice of this truth. There are those who seek truth outside the everyday life of this earth. There are others who find the joys and sorrows, the doubts and conflicts of this world to be established in truth; they do not seek truth in anything else. But we do not know this world if we see it as complete in itself. We know it only when we see its truth to be something that permeates and yet transcends it. Nothing is to be rejected, but all things are to be seen as established in the Ultimate which gives them the truth they have.

The world needs actors, but it also needs those who can see. I have felt within me this urge to see, and the need to give it an undying form in my creation. This seeing is not an idle whiling away of time, for in its beat the universe happens. No truth, however powerful, can establish itself unless it appeals though love and warmth. There is going on an immense preparation so that a song is born out of sound, a picture out of lines in order that we may come to like and love what we see. We forget what a wonder all this is. I have been called in the quarters that lie outside the business of everyday life to declare this wonder.

What Tagore is saying is Upanisadic, and yet it is essentially his own. He was one of those rare souls who could hold on to distinctions, and yet view all things as part of one and the same reality. He denied nothing, neither unity nor multiplicity, neither the ultimate sameness of things nor their phenomenal difference; as he said, 'I want to let go of nothing, I am complete only through it all'. Tagore was a poet, not a conventional spiritual aspirant, and as a poet it was his job to see it all in its ambiguity, richness, complexity and subtlety. So alive were his sensibilities that he could feel with equal intensity both the romantic beauty and fulfilment of love and its almost inevitable frustration and even the co-existence of such feelings; both the delight and the despair of being human, the sadness and the beauty of being parted from one's beloved, the charm and the ugliness of this world, both man's nearness to God and his distance from Him. He could do this because of the complex and rich ambiguities of his own nature which kept alive his sense of wonder and his sensitivity to the nuances of changing human feelings, in the poignancy of despair and in the freedom of delight.

A word here about including songs in this selection. Tagore broke away from the classical tradition of Indian vocal music where the melodic structure is all important and where words have only an accessory role, if any at all. In his music (in the creation of which he drew not only on the classical tradition but also on devotional and folk music and even on European music) the lyrical quality of the poetry is just as important as the melody. Tagore composed his melodies with their distinctive tune and timing specifically to fit the lyrics. As melodies they compare very poorly indeed with the traditional melodic structures of classical music; they appear thin, bare, even simplistic. But seen as the habitation of the lyrics they come surprisingly alive; the process is of mutual enrichment. The music is not great in itself but it has a certain haunting charm, at any rate for a Bengali who is a part of the environment and the mood the words convey. Since half the value of Tagore music lies in the lyrical quality of Tagore songs considered as poetry, I have included them here as illustrations of this quality. There is no reason why one cannot experiment with western melodies to see if they fit the songs.

One of the charges against Tagore, apart from mysticism and sugariness, has been his repetitiveness. This is to be expected in some degree in everyone who writes a geat deal; in one so prolific as Tagore it is inevitable. Admitting though that the same themes recur in different places, there is enough variety, a surprising amount, to keep translators busy and what has so far been done does no more than scratch the surface. Tagore has other faults as well. No writer is uniformly great and he was not either. Vagueness of thought and looseness of construction appear here and there spoiling an otherwise perfect stanza. Occasionally the tone sounds like preaching and emotion appears forced; at least not wholly sincere. Some poems are too long, they say too much, a few too ornamental. One can go on adding to this list. But in spite of all this his poetry achieves a height that is not too common an occurrence. I shall consider my labours justified if I have been able to convey some measure of this height in my translations.

SONGS

♣ The sky is filled with stars and the sun,
this earth with life vibrant.
Amongst it all I too have received a home
out of this wonder my song is born.
In the rhythm of ebb and tide of eternal time
the world floats,
its pull enters the blood stream
that through my nerves flows.
Out of his wonder my song is born.
I have trodden on grass passing through the wood
my mind infused with the surprise that the smell of flowers brings,
spread around me are such delightful gifts.
I have lent my ears, opened my eyes,
on the bosom of this earth poured forth my life,
looking for the unknown in all that I know.
This wonder brings forth my song.

♣ The summer breeze this early morn
stirs gentle and soft.
It brings to my mind the rhythm
of footsteps well-known.
A dream ends, and through the window
wafts in waves
bakul's sudden scent,
lightly touching the fringe
of my half-sleeping state.
The breeze this summer's morn
brings sweet happiness,
like the touch of loosened hair
come over in a caress.
The *champa* flower in the garden trembles
and in my heart mingles
and heart-throb
once felt in another morn.

Bakul–Small scented flowers, like stars in appearance.
Champa–A mildly scented flower, yellow in colour, that blooms in a middle-sized
    tree.

3

♣ Shadows of *ashad* cloud play around the *kadamba* grove,
the *piyal* trees swing in the wind in a dance pose.
From wood to wood passes a thrill
at the touch of the rain drop.
Lonely, my mind opens its wings
towards the far off.
The geese fly through the sky
what is it that inspires their speed?
The stormy flapping of their wings creates a wave
of melody in the east wind.
In this rainy evening, full of the cricket's call
somebody appears as if by stealth
in my heart, (in the midst of it all).
On my pain he lets fall his feet
in many a form.

♣ The rain falls in profusion
drip-drop all day long,
this day of the advanced rainy season.
The sky is burst open,
the overflow rushes on.
Now and again in the *sal* forest
the storm shakes as it roars,
and the water runs through the meadow
in a zig-zag course.
In the sky you can see someone dance
with flying clouds for his matted locks, massed.
My mind is let loose by this rain,
it is seized by the storm;
and my heart, full,
reaches for someone unknown.
Within me is a tumult, of doors opening up,
awakening the 'mad one' in the heart;
and someone is surely drunk
out there as in here.

Ashad – The third month of the Bengali year, beginning of the rainy season.
kadamba – A round yellow flower with a mild scent, blooms in the rainy season.
Piyal – A big tree.
Sal – A familiar tree in West Bengal, big in size.

4

♣ My mind keeps company with clouds
from horizon to horizon,
through limitless void, amidst this music
of *sravana* downpour,
ringing rimjhim, rimjhim, rimjhim.

My mind is with the wings of the geese
startled suddenly by the lightning beam,
when the rainstorm clatters in violent pleasure
– like jingling bells –
and the stream babbles on;
thaty is an invitation
to delight in destruction.
The wind blows from the eastern sea
into the rippling river waves
that, joyfully, swell and break.
My mind runs with their mad course
to the palm and the *tamala* forest,
whose branches, aggrieved, agitate.

♣ My day ends this eager rainy evening
amidst a thick flow from dense clouds.
My heart to overflowing fills
with the tune of water splashing under the shadow of trees.
From time to time in rumbling beats
a bass drum plays from sky to sky.
I feel as if someone from afar
has come near,
and he is waiting
silently behind this dark screen.
On his bosom plays a garland
threaded with the pain of parting,
a parting that still holds the sweet scent
of a scret meeting.
I feel that I can recognize his footsteps,
but I am baffled by this, his unfamiliar dress.

Sravana – The fourth month of the Bengali new year when the monsoon rain is
    heavy and continuous.
Tamala – A big dark tree.

5

♣ At the end of the monsoon night
today the early light of the dawn
mixes
with the soft black of the nimbus cloud.

In the bamboo bush from top to top
the leaves are touched with colour.
In its flow my heart gets lost
it is carried away, who knows where.

This sparkling of grass in a golden wave,
my heart's tremblings mix with it
in the same beat.
In love of this earth, and dyed in its light
my blood wells up in delight
and my mind, in the same mood
with the wood, bursts out in laughter.

♣ You did come,
but it was not a real coming
you made me understand
as you found your way back.
You passed by through a road that runs right in the front,
letting fall fleeting shadows.
This indifference of yours, I do not know if it was for real,
your restless feet spread pain all over the grass.
It was a time when from the leaves water fell in drops,
as if the green forest land found itself in tears.
You went in a slow pace, the air was then wet,
at the back, among the rows of *nipa* plants, played light and shade.

6

♣ This rainy day moves on
  into the approaching darkness of apprehension.
  And this enchanting evening deceives
  in the hope of an impossible union.
  Solitude deepens with the advancing night.
  Alas! my lamp looks out in vain,
  troubling the void around with a futile question.
  From nowhere comes a response,
  the mad wind, homeless, runs amok.
  All hope lost in deep darkness,
  the troubled night seeks some language
  in the dripping sound of rain,
  in wet *malati's* scent.

♣ You have come, the bewitcher of my eyes.
  What beauty do I see as I open up my sight!
  The bewitcher of my eyes, you have come,
  treading on heaps of fallen flowers,
  under the *sewli* tree, by its sides,
  on grass wet with dew –
  your feet dyed with the reddish hue
  of early sunlight.
  Light and shade look like the end of a sari and roll on from wood to
        wood,
  flowers look at one another and engage in silent speech.
  We wish to welcome you, remove the covering that hides your face,
  push away with both hands this slight cloud curtain.
  The goddess of the wood blows a conch
  from door to door in a deep tone.
  From string to string on the *veena* of the sky,
  hear a melody of welcome.
  Somewhere a golden dance bell sounds
  it could be in my heart.
  The bewitcher of my eyes, you have come
  pouring honey on all feelings, all works.

Malati – A creeper that blooms in the evening during the rainy season.
Sewli – A scented white flower on orange stalk.
Veena – A string instrument with frets, used since ancient times.

7

♣ In this *sarat* sun, as the morning dream ends,
I do not know what my heart is seeking.
What sort of call is it that comes from the *sefali* branch
and what song is the bird couple singing?

Today, in this delicious wind, my heart is restless,
the mind refuses to stay at home.
What flower is it that it is reaching for,
what smell is it in which it is enveloped,
as it runs towards the sky so blue?

Someone is not here this morning and life has lost its use.
I look around, my mind says, not this, not this, please.
In some land of dream, some shadowy heaven,
perhaps a woman, loose-haired, lives
She is crying today, in paid of having been parted,
in some grove, for me.

If, troubled in mind, I write a song,
who is there to hear it?
If I thread a garland from a basketful of flowers,
who is there to wear it?
If this life of mine I wish to offer,
at whose feet can I place it?
I am afraid lest I cause someone pain
through carelessness.

Sarat – The season after the rains when the sky shows a deep blue colour; season of the big religious festival called 'Durgapuja'.
Sefali – Another name for sewli; a scented white flower on orange stalk.

8

❀ I know that all is ready for you to go.
Yet, wayfarer, do tarry a while.
The rain falls in profusion from the *sravana* sky.
A line of trees fills the wood with shadow.
In the drip drop of water
I hear the cry, as it were,
of the *juthi* grove,
a cry that happens as the flowers drop.

Go, when the rains are over
and birds are singing everywhere,
when the goddess of the *sarat* season will arise
awakened by the sweet hymn of the *sewli* grove,
and the conch, sounding in white sunlight,
will imprint on her forehead an auspicious sign.

❀ My night spends itself out into this *sarad* morning,
tell me, flute, in whose hands should I leave you.
In your bosom has been sounding a welcome-farewell note for so
        long
in the morning and evening, in *falgun* and in *sravan*.
That which was in my mind, unnoticed,
you stole and made it into a song;
now its time is over, like a star at night's end,
so let it go and with *sewli* die a death.

Sravan – The fourth month of the Bengali year. The phrase 'sravan flow' is used as
    an expression for continuous downpour.
Juthi – A creeper with white scented flowers that blooms in the rainy season.
Sarat – The season after the rains when the sky shows a deep blue colour; season of
    the big religious festival called 'Durgapuja'.
Sewli – Scented white flower with orange stalk, blooms at the end of the rainy
    season.
Sarad – The autumnal season associated with the festival of Durgapuja, when
    special songs are sung to welcome the goddess Durga, songs which have a sad
    note as well, because Durga takes leave as soon as the festival is over.
Falgun – The beginning of spring when another version of the worship of the
    mother goddess takes place.
Sravan – The end of the rainy season when notes are already sounded of the
    impending arrival of Durga.
Sewli – Scented white flower with a saffron coloured stalk, blooms at the end of the
    rainy season.

9

♣ The month of *paush* is calling you,
come along in a hurry, come along.
Its basket today is full of ripe corn.
It is wonderful, beyond measure, it is wonderful.
The quarters behave as if drunk, on the paddy field,
through intoxication carried by the wind,
and gold from the sun spreads
all over on this earth's garment.
It is wonderful, beyond measure, it is wonderful.
The sky is delighted to hear
the flute that goes on playing in the meadow.
On a day like this, who can stop at home,
open up the door, please open up, do.
The dew touches the ear of the corn
and the laughter of light is born.
The joy of this earth knows no bound, it overflows.
It is wonderful, beyond measure, it is wonderful.

♣ Out of the fresh joy of *falgun*
I have fashioned a rhythm for my song.
The rows of trees in the wood
have brought to it the noisy call of the cuckoo,
have filled it with the smell of *bakul*.
The sacred charm of *madhabi*, honey-filled,
has dyed with colours the whole horizon.
My words have plucked the buds of *palas*
and tied them round your wrist.

Paush – The ninth month of the Bengali year; the time for winter harvest.
Falgun – The month that starts the season of spring.
Bakul – A big evergreen tree that has small scented flowers, like stars in appearance.
Madhabi – A scented flower that blooms in the summer and the rainy season.
Palas – A spring flower of red colour without scent.

♣ When the first buds appeared in the *mallika* grove
for you,my friend, I threaded a garland
to offer you with cupped hands.
The mist is still there on the forehead of the young dawn,
where the faint glow of the morning sun shimmers,
mixed with dew drops.
The song of the birds in the wood, my friend,
has not yet come to an end.
Do you have to go, now?
Oh, my sad creeper.
your tired *mallikas*
are about to drop.
The time for you to say your last say
as you bid farewell.

♣ Oh, dropped leaf,
I am on your side.
In many a laughter and many a tear
the spring has chanted the sacred formula of farewell
to my innermost ear.
Dropped leaf,
you have dressed yourself
in the colour of spring.
Is it because the stage is now set
for your last appearance?
You have played *holi*
with dust and with grass
in this last tale of spring's climax.
Let my veil, like yours, be dyed
with the colour of fire.
Let the setting sun touch
the last savings of my heart
with its magic stone.

Mallika-Scented white flower. Known as 'Bel' in colloquial Bengali.
Holi-A spring festival. According to the religious literature called the 'Puranas'
the origin of the festival lies in the play of Krishna with Radha-by throwing red
powder and coloured water at each other.

♣ Through this earth is flowing a stream of joy,
day and night, like nectar that overflows into
the endless sky.
The sun and the moon drink it by the handful
to keep their light, imperishable,
always bright.
The earth is full, ever, with life and light.
Why do you sit alone, wrapped up in yourself?
Why be so immersed in your selfish ends?
Look about and spread your heart around.
– Your small wounds, so insignificant, learn to disregard –
and fill its emptiness with love.

♣ Why is this murmuring sound today?
Why through the leaves of my trees in waves
pases a violet quake?
Some beggar must have come
to the door of my courtyard.
I fear he will ask for all
my mind, all my wealth.
My heart says he is familiar,
when he sings bloom my flowers.
Deep within me is heard
the footsteps of that traveller.
That's why, startled, my sleep is over.

♣ Do accept me this time, Lord, do,
do not turn away,
steal my heart and stay.
I do not wish to repeat those days
devoid of you,
let them finish in dust.
Now let my life open up in your light,
for ever alert.

I do not know what deluded me,
what promise lured me,
that I moved around hither and thither
on roads, amidst meadows.
Now bring your face near to my heart
and deliver a message, your own.

Many faults, many a deception
still lurk
secretly in my heart.
Do not turn me away any more for that,
Lord, purify them
in fire.

♣ The bee comes into my room and hums,
telling me of someone.
The light from the sky somewhere
has opened up the *madhabi* in the wood.
With news of this awakening it comes
as it hums all day long.
How can I stop at home, my mind is so restless.
How do I pass my day, doing nothing but wait.
It spreads enchantment and I forget about work,
as the bee weaves a net of melody,
telling me of someone.

Madhabi – A scented flower that blooms in the summer and the rainy season.

13

♣ Because you and I shall meet
the sky is full of light,
because you and I shall meet
the green earth is in delight.
Because you and I shall meet
the night, world in her lap, stays awake,
dawn arrives to open the door on the easter sky,
full with the music of bird song.
In this eternal current a boat floats
hoping for union,
flowers of many ages fill the basket of welcome
and overflow.
Because you and I shall meet,
my heart moves in readiness
in a bride's dress,
forever
looking for a suitor.

♣ This is not a sweet play
between you and me all day –
a lifelong play, that takes place
morning and evening –
not a sweet play.
Often light vanishes from sight,
often comes thundering the stormy night
and the troubled world plunges me
in a dense sea of doubt.
Time and again the dam bursts open,
flood sweeps through.
On a heart-rending day
everywhere there is lament.
Oh *Rudra*, let this message ring in my heart
through all my misery and happiness –
your love strikes one,
but it does not neglect.

Rudra – The destructive aspect of Siva is referred to by this name. But this
destruction is a prelude to well-being that Rudra also offers to those who can
take him.

♣ You do not know me, the real me.
She whom you love is a phantom.
It is round her neck,
that you place your garland.
Alas, that withers at every moment.
Light is fearful to come close,
wind stays at a distance
(lest its touch the illusion disclose).

Come suffering, burn your flame,
imprint on my forehead your fiery emblem.
Let death come in silence
revealing to me the ultimate.
Let all veil be lifted,
all defeat come to an end.

♣ You did not find me, you did not.
I sat absent minded in a corner,
the lamp had gone out.
You went away seeing no one.
You came to the door
and then forgot,
it would have opened had you knocked.
The boat of my fate ran aground
on this tiny rock.
On a stormy night I sat counting time,
but I failed to hear your chariot's sound.
Shuddering in the thunder's rumbling noise
I pressed my hands tightly round my breast.
In the sky the fiery flame of lightning
wrote a curse, then disappeared.

♣ Friend, write my name
in the temple of your mind
with love, in secret care.
A song is ringing in my heart,
learn how to play its beat
with the dance bells on your feet.
Retain in the courtyard of your palace,
in endearing caress
my noisy bird.
Remember, friend, to hold
in your bracelet of gold
the friendship thread
that comes from my wrist.
Pick with forgetfulness a flower from my creeper
and place it on your coiffure.
A dot of vermilion, auspicious,
wear that to decorate your forehead
in my fond remembrance.
The enchantment of my mind,
let its sweetness be spread
and mix with your body-scent
as you wrap it around.
Beloved, in your incomparable glory
receive in utter conquest
my eager life and death.

♣ Last night a song came to my mind,
you were then not with me.
That which I have been waiting, in silent tears,
all my life to tell you,
of a sudden it flashed in the dark
as a song in homage offered.
But you were then not with me.
I thought when the morning came
I would let you have the secret.
The scent of flowers, unattached, floats around
birds with their call fill the sky.
However much, with all my heart, I try,
the tune does not fit the words
now, when you are with me.

♣ The wind, indifferent, loosens the buds
which drop on its way;
I have picked them up and placed at your feet,
will you not hold them in your compassionate hands?
Tomorrow the buds will blossom in your lap
when I shall be gone.
Let your fingers, hurt,
as they thread a garland,
remember me in sweet pain.
The bird "Speak-beloved", sleepless,
spends itself this enchanted night
in sad, futile call.
The whisperings of two, love-lost,
float arond in moonlight
this April fullmoon night.
The hints of that will remain
in tomorrow's idle noon
as you thread through.

♣ My mind is restless,
Who knows, who knows for whom.
A bird on an unknown flight path called,
it called and went away
far into the horizon.
Stirred, my thoughts take to flight
in the wind,
in the wind from beyond the sea.
See, the goose of my dreams
is on its way, wings open,
who is it that bound me at home
in a golden cage?

♣ Your mind wavered as you left that evening
– the evening was far gone –
on your way to the door you turned your face
there was something in your thought.
You left with a smile in the corner of your eyes –
now I sit with a trembling heart, and wonder.
You are somewhere far.
In the sky a flock of cranes fly
with them my pain keeps company.
I wish to ask you just for once,
what was it that you did not say as you went.
It is to be found in the wet jasmine's pain
that spreads through its scent?

♣ There was a song in your *veena* and flowers in my basket,
the same south wind did swing us together that day.
A wave, of what nobody knows for certain, filled the atmosphere
as the boat of your melody dropped anchor in my coloured flower.
That day I thought that in the beat of your song
the blossoming of flowers in my heart will forever go on.
Yet the song floated away, the flower no longer bloomed at day's
end.
In the sweet play of the spring somewhere there was a mistake.

♣ This is a tearful spring, my friend, not come before
It has dyed my parting pain with the red colour of *kingsuk*
The wild *mallika* at the flower grove
with fresh leaves has got itself adorned.
It is wide-eyed day and night, living in expectation.
The south wind from the distance brings a song,
The song of a lonely separated soul,
and in my grove the flowers want
to tear off all their bonds.
I knock at this closed door of life
with anxious hands again and again.
I have not managed to give myself –
troubled with this pain.

Veena – An ancient string instrument with frets.
Kingsuk – A red spring flower.
Mallika – Scented white flower, known as 'Bel' in colloquial Bengali.

19

♣ Once, my beloved, you sat under this tree
in my garden
amidst the flowers.
Today, is that all forgotten?
But the river nearby which flows,
since before time we know,
remembers it all.
In its stream, curving as it flows,
the line of your braided hair shows.
On its bank are your footsteps,
as if there faintly printed.
Today, is all that an illusion,
or have you forgotten?
The melody you used to sing many a day
as you sat there by yourself,
through the grass even now spreads
from time to time when it shakes.
You used to sit in the shade
and thread a garland
with flowers held
in a portion of your sari at the end.
Spring is still looking for that touch –
a honeyed touch that gladdens –
in the *champa* flower.
Today, is all this for you a deception,
or have you forgotten?

Champa – A flower that blooms in a middle-sized tree, scented, mildly coloured
(yellow being the most usual).

20

♣ The night is dark, the confidant is alert,
empty stand woods and groves.
The noisy wind blows round her solitary home
where the sad maiden, separated, sits.
The stars shine in the deep blue sky,
Jamuna sings merrily on (earth).
The trees murmur, the springs spatter,
the creepers grow full of flowers.
With expectant eyes at the path in the wood
stares the agitated girl,
she sees nothing and turns her eyes
back to the threading of wild flowers.
Suddenly *Radha* is startled, eagerly she looks,
she throws the garland away
saying, 'listen, oh friend, the flute plays,
Krishna has come at the grove'.
The dark night wakes up, in the far distance
plays the flute in a fine tune,
Jamuna, youthful, mixes with it her song
as gurgling she splashes on.
Bhanu says, 'listen, oh *Kanu*,
thirsty is *gopini's* heart,
your love is for her pure nectar
she will drink it with utter delight.'

Jamuna – A river of north India that is associated with the Radha-Krishna love
  story.
Radha – The lady-love of Krishna, the famous lover of Hindu mythology.
Krishna – One of the gods of the Hindu triad, also conceived as the supreme God
  who is the symbol of love. The Radha-Krishna love story is interpreted by the
  devotees as the best example of pure love.
Bhanu – The name of the poet who wrote many songs on the theme of
  Radha-Krishna love, and from whom Tagore borrowed his theme.
Kanu – Another name of Krishna.
Gopini – Here refers to Radha, generally means the cowherd women of Brindaban.

♣ There is nothing to stop me from getting lost
anywhere at all,
if it happens in the mind.
So I open up the wings of my song.
I go beyond the stony wilderness of fairy tales;
I lose my way and reach some far away place,
where silence reigns.
I get to know the *champa* flower in *parul's* grove
in my own mind.
There is nothing to stop me from getting lost,
anywhere at all
when the wings of my song are afloat.
As the sun sets in the horizon
masses of clouds look like flowers in the sky –
then mixing with the foam of seven seas,
I float away somewhere far off.
and in my mind I burst open the closed door
of a fairy home.

Champa – A scented flower of yellow colour that blooms in a middle-sized tree.
Parul – Classical name 'patali'. Parul is a flower that belongs exclusively to fairy
tales.

♣ When my footsteps will no longer be printed round here,
my ferryboat no longer ply at this station,
when all buying and selling are over,
all borrowing and lending,
finished all comings and goings to the market,
it does not then matter if you do not remember me
do not call out for me, as you look at the stars.

When dust will settle on the strings of the *tanpura*,
the doors will be covered with bramble,
the flower garden, the grassy lawn
will look like a jungle,
and moss will gather round the edge of the pond,
it does not then matter if you do not remember me,
do not call out for me, as you look at the stars.

The flute will then play in this corner of the earth
as it does today.
The day will go on, just the same, as it does now.
The ferryboat will be filled
at each station.
The cow will graze, the cowherd boy play in the meadow,
it does not then matter if you do not remember me,
do not call out for me, as you look at the stars.

But who says that in that morning I will not be there?
In all this play this very me will be playing.
I shall be called by a new name,
embraced by a fresh pair of arms.
But I shall come and go, the eternal me.
It does not then matter if you do not remember me,
do not call out for me, as you look at the stars.

Tanpura – A drone instrument of four strings, used as an accompaniment in singing, especially classical singing.

POEMS

An Awakening

I know now that the night's dream
has come to an end.
From the garland the flowers have gone,
what remains is but the thread.
No longer is there the secret look,
the stealthy advance, the play at turning back.
The eyes are there, not in them
love's obsession.
The arms twined round mine
are now only a bond.

The smile which used to play
round your lips
is no longer to be seen.
No longer is there the attempt
at hide and seek.
The voice which used to send your
heart into a flutter,
and through your body a wave of pleasure
no longer does.
A song no longer brings
tears to the eyes,
which bashfulness tries to hide.

The flute played,
I gave in,
and that was the end.
What remains is a shackle
round my feet –
a noose to hang with.
The abundant night is now past
and its memory can only bring
shame to my heart.
Happiness is gone, not its pretence.
What is left behind is but an attempt
at caress without any sense.

(Abridged)
(Manasi)

27

Journey To An Unknown Destination

How much further will you take me
you of beauty endearing?
Tell me at which port will drop anchor
this golden boat you are steering?
Whenever I ask you, lady from some foreign part,
sweet-smiling, you only smile,
I fail to understand what you have in mind.
What does your move suggest?
You point your finger in silence
to the overflowing water, endless,
to the sun at one end of the sky '
going down in the west.
What is it we shall find there?
Why are we travelling, in which quest?

Tell me, I ask you, you stranger,
Over there, where the day at evening's call
is burning itself out in a funeral pyre
and waves are flashing like liquid fire
on the backdrop of the molten sky,
where quarters appear
as if about to shed tears,
is that where you live?
Beyond the wave-torn sea,
at the foot of the cloud-kissed hill
where the setting sun disappears?
You smile, looking at my face,
but not a word about where the boat veers.

The wind moans in a constant sigh,
the heaving wave roars in a passion high.
The deep blue water is anguished;
I look round, no bank is to be found,
as if limitless tears flood this earth
and then quiver.

Yet, there plies this golden boat,
there the still-glowing evening rays float.
Why do you sit amidst it all
in a silent laughter?
It is beyond me to tell why in it you take
so much pleasure.

"Who will come with me"?
When first you had called
I looked at your eyes
on a fresh morn.
You spread your hands westwards to show
the boundles ocean that there flows,
where restless light shimmers
like hope in some breast.
I boarded and asked:
Does new life await,
does hope's dream reap there
a golden harvest?'
You looked and smiled,
as before, silent.

Since then, clouds have gathered at times,
at times has arisen with sun.
Now the sea was rough, now it looked
a tranquil picture.
Time goes past, the sail moves in the wind,
the golden boat has disappeared, I find.
In the west, the sun descends
towards its hillside rest.
Let me ask you once again:
does soothing death here await,
is there peace, can one find sleep,
under this dark's breast?
You smile, only your eyes are alive,
there is silence for the rest.

Soon the dark night will spread its wings
and arrive.
The golden light will disappear
from the evening sky.

Now remains only your body scent,
the splashing of water's current.
Your hair, wind-swept
on my body flies.
And when heart fluttering, body benumbed,
anxiously I shall call you and ask,
where are you, come close
let me feel your touch,
you will not speak, and I shall not see
even your silent smile.

(Sonar Tari)

A Circle

The incense wants to be one with the scent,
the scent to wrap itself round the incense.
Melody wants to take shape in rhythm,
rhythm turns to melody instead,
feeling looks for a body in form,
form can only find itself in feeling.
The infinite seeks the intimate presence of the finite,
the finite to disappear in the infinite.
I do not know whose scheme this is
in the eternal cycle of beginning and end
that between feeling and form should be this interchange,
that the bound should be on a search after freedom –
freedom asking to be housed in the bound.

(Utsarga)

A Brahman

(*A story based on the Chandogya Upanisad*)

Amidst the dark shadows of the forest,
on the bank of *saraswati*
the evening sun has set.
The sons of *rishis* have returned
to the quiet *asram*, carrying wood
from a distance on their head.
The tired cows with cool, calm eyes,
have returned with them
to the forest hermitage.
Their evening bath taken, the boys sit together
around *guru* Gautam
in the courtyard of the cottage,
where fire burns for *homa* sacrifice.
High above in the endless sky eternal peace reigns,
rapt, as it were, in meditation.
There clusters of stars appear
like attentive disciples, sitting in rows,
noiseless, eager to learn.
Suddenly the solitary *asram* is startled
as it resounds to Gautam's voice,
'my sons, now attend, I speak of Brahma'.
At this moment enters a young boy
to this courtyard,
carrying a handful of offerings.
Fruits and flowers placed at the lotus feet of the sage
in greeting,
devotional obeisance done, he says,
'Your Reverence, I am come for initiation,
desiring Brahma knowledge.
My home is in Kusakshetra, my name Satyakama'.
Hearing this, the sage, with a soothing smile on his face,
replies in soft affection,

Saraswati – A river of ancient India mentioned in the Rigveda.
Rishi – A learned spiritual aspirant and teacher, also name for a composer of Vedic hymns. A noble character.
Asram – A residence of holy men in ancient India, usually in a forest.
Homa – Vedic sacrifice performed with offerings of clarified butter in fire whilst hymns are chanted.

31

'I wish you well, my boy, what is your lineage?
Only a brahman has right to this sacred knowledge'.
In a slow speech the boy replies,
'Your Reverence, I have no knowledge.
If you permit, tomorrow, when I have asked my mother,
I shall come back'.
So saying he touches again the feet of the sage
and returns
through a dark path
flanked by rows of trees,
to his mother's cottage
that stands on the edge of a silently sleeping village,
on the sand bank.

At home the evening light burns.
His mother, Jabala, waits at the door
looking out for Satyakama.
She takes the returning boy to her bosom
and murmuring words of blessing
places a kiss on his head.
Satyakama asks,
'Tell me mother,
What is the name of my father?
Of what lineage am I born?
Today I went to guru Gautam, desirous of initiation.
The guru's words to me were
that only a brahman had right
of access to supreme knowledge.'
At this Jabala's head bends
and she says in a mother's soft voice,
'In my youth I was poor,
in attendance on many men,
when you were born.
You are the child of Jabala,
without a husband.
My son, your lineage is not known'.

Next day the dawn breaks,
fresh, content,
on the head of trees in the forest.
The hermit boys look like young light,
bathed in soothing dew,

around them hovers a glow of refreshing virtue
that sentiments of devotion produce.
They sit circling guru Gautam
under the shadow of the old banyan tree.
The guru's locks are still wet from his morning bath.
A gentle picture, he shines bright like a figure of peace and purity.
In the courtyard the birds chirp, the bees hum,
the sound comes of splashing water,
and mixing with these arise
the tranquil *sama* chant,
deep, delectable,
sung in a beautiful chorus
of a variety of young voices.

At this moment Satyakama enters.
Obeisance done to the guru's feet
he stands in silence,
opening widely his noble eyes.
A blessing is uttered by the teacher,
and then he asks,
'I am pleased to see you, but tell me dear boy,
what is your lineage?'
The boy lifts up his head and replies,
'Your Reverence, I still do not know.
My mother said she was on attendance on many men
when I was born to her without a husband.
My lineage is not known'.

The effect of this news on the boys present
is like the scattering of restless insects
that takes place when a beehive is stoned.
They begin whispering, struck by surprise.
Some laugh, some heap abuse
on this shameless non-aryan for his pride.
Guru Gautam alone leaves his seat and stands,
embracing the boy with open arms
and says, 'You are not a non-brahman, my boy,
you are amongst the best of the twice-born,
your lineage is truly noble'.   *(Chitra)*

Sama – Name for Vedic chanting and singing of hymns that occur in a particular
    Veda called the 'Sama Veda'. It is said to be the origin of Indian music. (It is
    supposed that only three notes were used for Sama chanting.)

An Old Servant

In appearance like a ghost, he was extremely stupid.
Whenever anything was missing, the wife said, 'Kesta must be the
thief'.
I abused him at every step, it went through one ear and out the
other,
he got more punishment than money, yet he never seemed to wake
up.
I used to call at the height of my voice crying. 'Kesta', whenever an
urgent need arose,
I hurried and scurried and even if I searched the whole country no-
one was to be found.
If I gave him three of something, he kept one but nobody knew
where the rest went.
If I gave him only one thing that into three pieces he promptly
made.
He could go to sleep at any place any time during the day
and when I called him names, 'You wicked fool, wretched',
he stood by the door and smiled, which made my blood boil.
Yet to give up being attached to him was difficult, his standing
with us was many years old.
The lady of the house often got furious, 'I shall give up and go,
leave all this to you, you may with Kesta make your home.
He is immune to rebuke, all things, food, clothes,
utensils, furniture, he spoils
and because of him money is being spent like water.
If he goes to the market you can be sure not to see him again the rest
of the day.
Is it possible that no other servant could be found even if one had
tried?'
At this I would get very angry and fetch him by his top-knot, quick,
and say, 'get out, right now, I am giving you the sack'.
He would slowly depart and I would think, 'it is done at last', next
day I would find him,
standing with the hubble-bubble in his hand, How stupid!
He had a smiling face, there was no complaint in his untroubled
mind,

34

well, if he would not go even when sacked, there was nothing to be
    done with this servant of old.

That year I received some money as a bonus through agency work.
I figured that to *Sri Brindavan* for a pilgrimage I would go.
My wife wanted to come too, I tried to make her see
that a wife automatically shared the religious merit of the husband,
    otherwise it became expensive.
Well, there was some argument but with ropes all sorts of packets
    were tied;
with her bangles jingling she arranged the suitcase and cried,
'You will have a lot of trouble with Kesta in an unfamiliar place'.
I said, 'you are mistaken, Nivaran is coming with me instead'.
The train was on its way, when I got down at Burdwan (an
    in-between station) I found,
who else but Kesta, with a smiling face, hubble-bubble in hand.
How much of his insolence did I have to stand and for how long?
But however much I blamed him I was secretly pleased that the old
    servant had come along.
We got off at *Sridham*, at right and left, back and front
priest-guides flocked for custom, making life unbearable.
Six or seven of us got together and in great friendship
we rented a house. I thought my days here would pass in ease.
Alas! I saw nothing of the *gopis*, the gardens or anything of
    Krishna.
I had hoped to find eternal spring, now I was dying of *basanta*.
Like a dream event, in a hurry the friends at once left the place.
My body spotted all over with pox, I was left to fend for myself.
I would call night and day, in a pitiful feeble voice, 'Kesta come
    here.
It took me all this time to visit a foreign place, and the result I die'.

Sri Brindavan – A place of pilgrimage situated on the west of the river Jamuna.
    Famous as the place where the love-play between Radha and Krishna of the
    Puranas (Hindu Religious literature) took place.
Sridham – Any pilgrimage place in India that is thought to be inhabited by a god or
    goddess.
Gopi – A woman of the Ahir tribe who lived in Brindaban. According to Hindu
    myths these women were romantically drawn to Krishna who danced his
    famous Rasa dance with them.
Basanta – Bengali name for Pox. It is so named because the disease happens during
    the season of Basanta (spring).

To look at his face was an assurance, as if he was a great treasure.
He would stand day and night by my side, this old servant of mine,
    with pleasure.
He brought me water, wished me well, with his hands soothed my
    head.
He stood there, quite unmoving, without much sleep or food.
He would say again and again, 'Master, have no fear, listen
I am sure you would go home and see *mathakurun*, again'.
Well, I did get well and was up but by then to Kesta it had come,
on his own body he had to take this, my dreadful disease.
Two days passed, with Kesta unconscious, then his pulse failed.
I tried to get rid of him often, this time he really went.
After some days, at the end of the pilgrimage, I went home.
That day my faithful companion was not to be found with me any
    more.

(Chitra)

Mathakurun-'Ma' literally means mother. This is a respectful address that a
    servant uses for his or her mistress, suggesting her role as a mother in relation to
    all dependents.

Two Acres of Land

I was left with only two acres of land, the rest swallowed up in debt.
The squire said, 'You know, Upen, I have made up my mind to buy
 it'.
I replied, 'You are a landlord with no end of possession,
look, what I have got is barely enough to die on'.
At this the *raja* said, 'well, you know I have recently acquired a
 garden,
it will be equal in length and breadth with these two acres added.
You will have to give it up'. I said, tearfulness spreading through
 my breast,
my eyes wet, 'Be kind enough to save this poor man's family
 residence.
The land where seven generations had lived is valued more than
 gold.
Am I so God-forsaken as to have to sell it because of debt?'
The *raja*'s eyes went red, and for a while he kept silent,
the smiling a cruel smile said, 'We shall see what happens'.

A month and a half later I was turned out of my home on to the
 road.
The land was sold under a decree of debt on a false pretext, of
 course.
It seems those who have things galore want them even more,
the hands of the king steal the meagre wealth of the poor.
Thought I – well God perhaps wants me to forego all attachment to
 this world,
that's why he has exchanged for me the whole universe for two
 mere acres of land.
So I turned a mendicant, by becoming a disciple of a wandering
 holyman.

And I saw many a charming place, many sceneries beautiful.
But wherever I went, on land or on sea, in a town or in seclusion,
I could not forget, night or day, those two acres of land I lost.
Well, I wandered around in market towns, in meadows and on
 river banks for upwards of fifteen years,

Raja – literally means 'king of a small kingdom'. Here used for a big landlord
whose power is like that of a king as far as the village poor are concerned.

37

then one day, for returning home, I was suddenly possessed of a
  great urge.

I bow to you again and again, you are beautiful, Bengal, my
  mother land,
your wind blows gently on *Ganga*'s bank to cool the heat in my
  heart,
your meadows endlessly expand, the brow of the sky kisses the dust
  at your feet,
shadow-sheltered, your little villages are tiny abodes of peace.
Your mango groves, where cowherd boys play, are dense with
  leaves.
The black water of your still ponds is like soothing affection that
  the night brings.
The Bangali housewife, her bosom full of love, carries back home
  her pitcher,
one is impatient to call her mother, to see her one's eyes fill with
  tears,
In a couple of days, in the second period of the noon, I entered my
  own village
leaving the potter's house on the right, on the left the ground where
  the chariot festival takes place.
I went beyond *hatkhola*, the place where was *Nandi's* barn, soon
  leaving behind the village shrine.
Full of thirst, I came at last near the place where once was my own
  house.
Fie on you, fie a thousand times, my land, you shameless whore,
you can belong to whoever owns you – an act so unlike a mother!
Can you still remember those days when you were a poor man's
  land,
the days when you held in your garment lots of ordinary greens,
  fruits, flowers?
Why have you on today this luxurious dress, for those enchantment?
On your garment five-coloured leaves are printed, on your hair
  special flowers placed.
For you I have turned a mendicant, without home or happiness.
You sit here in luxury and, like a witch, in laughter spend your
  days,
proud of a rich man's care. Have your really become so different

Ganga – A famous river of India that runs through many provinces of the north.
Hatkhola – A place where the weekly market of the village takes place.
Nandi – A Hindu surname.

that no a hint of those days had anywhere been left?
You were then a figure of bliss, the remover of hunger, full of sweet
    love.
However much you laugh today, however much dress up,
you were then a goddess, now no more than one who serves.

Broken hearted I turned round and round and glanced everywhere.
Lo! there still stood the same old mango tree near the wall.
I sat under it and wept and this took away some of my pain.
One by one came to my mind memories of my young days.
I remembered I could hardly go to sleep on a stormy night one
    Jaistha
for one had to get up early and run to pick up fallen mangoes.
Then there used to be the delicious silent noon and truancy from
    school,
I was sad to think that all that from my life was forever gone.
Suddenly the wind breathed, some branches of the tree swung
and two ripe fruits dropped on the ground, right beside my lap.
I thought I was being recognized by my motherlike land at long
    last,
and I bowed down my head paying reverence to the gift that her
    affection had brought.

Exactly then ran towards me the gardener looking like a messenger
    of death,
an inhabitant of *Orissa*, his hair tied up in a bun, he began to abuse
    in a high note.
Said I, 'I have given up my all without protest.
What a fuss that I now claim only two fruits from that'.
The man did not know me, he dragged me on placing his bamboo
    stick on my shoulder,
to where the squire was fishing, rod in hand, with his companions.
Hearing the tale he fumed in anger and said, 'I would beat you to
    death'.
And whatever he said was blown up by his hangers-on a
    thousandfold.

I replied, 'Sir, I do no more than beg two pieces of fruit'.
The squire mocked in laughter, 'here is a seasoned thief in the
    guise of a mendicant'.
I smiled amidst tears and thought 'what a fate,
you, sir, have today turned virtuous, and I am accused of theft!'

Orissa – A province of India adjacent to West Bengal.   *(Chitra)*

A Resolution

I shan't become an ascetic, I shan't.
They will blame me, I can see.
I tell you, I shan't become one, unless
I find a lady to renounce with me.

I have taken a vow, I shall not relent –
if I do no find a *bakul* grove to sit in,
do not find a mind after my heart and win it,
I shant't become a renouncer, I shan't
unless there be a lady beside me,
sitting in penance as an ascetic.

I shan't leave home and wander around,
indifferent as a mendicant,
if nobody smiles a charming smile
that makes you forget the world.
If the end of her blue sari does not flap
restless in a gentle breeze,
if jungling sounds do not enter my mind
from bangles on her wrist,
I shan't become an ascetic, I tell you, I shan't,
unless there be a lady with me doing her penance.

I shan't become an ascetic, I promise you,
if at the end its power
fails to help me create a new world
that has a brand new heart.
If with a tune in my *veena*
I cannot make someone
forget all decorum and look at me with eyes
that say they will be mine
I shan't become an ascetic, I shan't,
if there be no lady with me to do her penance.

(Kshanika)

Bakul – A large evergreen flower tree, also its sweet scented flower.
Veena – An ancient musical instrument.

40

The Day's End

A falling-down inn.
Through the cracked foundation
the fig tree grows,
spreading branches around.
On the hot road in the intense sun
I have spent the day somehow or other,
hoping I shall find room at the inn,
when I get to it in the evening.
Darkness falls on the meadow,
the village folks return home,
I arrive here to find
there is nobody about.

They came here through many ages
at the end of many days
to stop and wash their dusty feet
before taking rest.
On a moonlit night they sat
in the soothing, cool courtyard.
They told one another
stories of many lands.
The bird song in the morning
brought them new life,
when the trees swung (in the wind)
through the weight of flowers.

The day I came here
the lamp was not lighted.
Some black marks of old flames
on the floor I found painted.
Towards the bush on the dried-up pond's bank
glow-worms veer,
bamboo branches on the broken path
throw shadows of fear.
At this end of my journey
I have become the guest of nobody!
Alas, my long, lonely night.
Alas, my tired shadow.   (Kheya)

41

A Gift

Beloved, what gift should I bring you
this morning
with my own hands?
Should it be a morning song?
The morning grows tired in the hot sun
like a flower on a stalk,
and song, exhausted,
comes to an end.

My friend, what do you wish for
at the end of the day,
as you come to my door?
Is it the evening lamp?
This lamp is for the lonely corner
of a still house.
Do you wish to take it in the crowd
as you journey on?
Alas!
it will be blown out in the wind
on your road,

What resource do I have to offer you a present.
Whether it is flower or a garland
is of no consequence;
they will surely become dry,
lose colour and be reduced to pieces.
What I myself place in your hands
will slip off your relaxed fingers
in forgetfulness.
and, mixing with dust, will there disappear.

Better that, when there is time
for a moment,
you will amble along my garden
rather absentminded,
and suddenly standing still,

surprised by the pleasure of an unknown
scent somewhere hidden,
will get lost, that gift,
that will be yours.
Your eyes will suddenly be seized with illusion,
and you will see
as if from the evening's coiffure
drops a coloured light
and trembling that touches
your dream, like a magic stone.
That light, that unknown gift
will be yours.

What is best in me appears in sudden bursts
and then disappears.
It has no name,
its tune causes a stir on its way,
and then its startled dance bells
are no more.
I do not know the way to it.
Hands do not reach there nor do words.
Friend, what you will yourself gather from there,
through your own emotion,
that gift, come-unawares, unasked-for,
is yours.
What I can offer you is nothing in comparison,
be it a flower or a song.

(Balaka)

The New Year

The tired, withered night of the old year
has just finished, oh! traveller.
The burning sun invites you on the way
with the song of *Rudra*, the terrible.
From distance to distance
in its sharp tune the narrow road winds,
as if it were the one-stringed instrument
of a wandering mendicant.

Oh! traveller,
let the dust of the grey road
be your sustainer,
the whirlwind wrap you round its breast
like a moving garment
tear you away from all your bond
to take you to the horizon's end and beyond.

Not for you the wellbeing of home,
the evening light, the tear of love.
In your path awaits the blessing of the summer storm
of the thunder that roars on a rainy night..

*   *   *

It invites you to a thorny bend
awaiting like the hidden hood of a serpent.
all loss you will face
like a gift, invisible, priceless.
The immortality that you crave
is not pleasure, nor comfort,
it is not peace or rest.
You will be chased by death,
that is for you *Rudra*, the terrible's grace.

Abridged - (Balaka)

Rudra - In the religious literature of the Hindus called 'Puranas' Siva, in his role as
the God of destruction, is also called Rudra. The Rigvedic Rudra is conceived
somewhat differently from the Puranic Rudra.

44

Last Spring

My desire has to come true before the day's end
otherwise, I fear, it will be too late -
   We shall go and pick
   fallen flowers of spring
   together, just for once, my friend.
At your flower beds, spring will come again and again,
only one of these, as I stand at your door, I beg.

Time has gone past, much of it a waste
careless I have made no haste.
   Suddenly in your eyes
   in this darkening light
   I find not much of it is left.
That is why like a spendthrift, I sit counting,
with anxious diffidence, these last days of spring.

Do not, my friend, be apprehensive.
Amidst your trees, with flowers so ready to please,
   I shall not linger for more than a while.
   Shall not even turn back my eyes
   as I say good-bye, when it is time to leave.
Your eyes I shall not look into, hoping for a tear
to keep alive with tender thoughts a memory so dear.

Do not turn back, I pray, just yet,
the light lingers on, the sun has not set.
   A little time for us is there still.
   "we must not steal it like a thief"
   no need yet to be troubled by this thought.
Let, from behind the leaves,the declining light
shine in your black hair for a little while.

I would like to hear you laugh, a sweet laugh but loud
in an uncalled-for exuberance spread so heartlessly around
   that by the wood's pond a timid squirrel
   will suddenly feel fearful
   and started it will bound.

45

I shall not then whisper to bring back what is past,
shall not ask to slow down your restless feet to make it last.

Then it is time for you to leave
tramping hastily on dry leaf,
    when the returning birds in their flocks
    raise everywhere an indistinct call
    and bestow on this day's end a troubled feel.
In this evening thick with bamboo bush shade will vanish your
      image,
as at the cow-dust hour the last tune on the flute is played.

(Purabi)

Last stanza omitted

The Ever-moving

The futile cry 'no, don't go'
whom does it call back,
where is the bond
that will turn the boundless into the bound?

The world is like a flooded passage,
its current speeds towards the other side
carrying all in a heap
in laughter and tear.
On the sea of eternal time
restless shapes form and dissolve,
foaming with the loud cry of 'no, no'.
Mingled with that voice, amidst the endless sky,
resounds the drum of God *Rudra* –
'no, no, no'.
Oh mind! let go all grief, greed and fear,
the river of creation runs on in currents of endless destruction.

Yes, everything shall pass away.
Yet I love –
and in a flash creation smiles
in an impulse of joy
amidst the very flow of destruction.
In the *veena* strings of death
take shape the song of life,
the endless stream of a fleeting grace.

From time to time flashes up the flame of eternity,
illuminating the mirage of the moment.
In the bottomless flow of tears is carried
the mother's soft affection,
the lovers' exchange of heart.

Rudra – In the religious literature of India called the "Puranas" Siva, the God of
destruction is also called Rudra. Siva means 'auspicious', Rudra, 'terrible'.
Rudra-siva means 'the auspicious-terrible God'.
Veena – A string instrument with frets used since ancient times.

47

And in the proud courage of the hero
in the playfield of vanishing life,
is treasured the beauty of this earth.

The infinite leaves its gift
in the palm of the passing, its measure
lies not in time's duration.
It remains great,
whether it lasts or not through ages.

Treasure it as long as it endures even at the cost of life.
When the chariot of farewell speeds on its way,
should 'victory' and leave free the passage,
forgetful of self.
The little earth that your life occupies,
what it is does or does not possess is a trivial question.
Within the bosom of the Immense
is contained all, in one form or another.

Leave behind the dark well of your little world,
look upwards to the limitless sky, to find
the bliss-form of *pralaya*.
Oh, you grief-stricken,
in the end the bubble of your grief
shall be swept away
in the ocean of peacefulness.

(Parisesh)

Pralaya – According to Hindu cosmology time is cyclical and this cycle is composed of phases of destruction and creation following one another without beginning or end. Each phase lasts a long time, 12000 god-years. Pralaya represents the phase of destruction.

Consolation

You, miserable man,
the weight of the dumb pain
you are carrying will find no relief.
No help exists anywhere, futile prayer
can only add to the poverty of one's heart.

You, dumb earth,
it is a wonder
that your breast is not torn asunder
having constantly to bear
the burden of this world,
sorrowful and sad.

You, dumb tree,
you take on your head
the cruel heat of summer;
bear patiently
the impact of the endless floods
that the rainy season
lets loose on earth.

It makes me think.
All trial, all suffering
will go down without a trace
to the wide breast
of this earth,
whose dark interior,
deep, cool, silent
is for ever swallowing up
the poison
that time churns up.

And at the end of this disappearance
what you will find is green grass,
noiseless, tender.
Undulating night and day.

All loss, all wound that death creates
are there altogether absent.
There the *Vanaspati* tree, tranquil, grave
raises its head toward sunrise,
And in the cup of its leaves
bloom flowers
like a crown of glory
for this earth.

Dumb earth, dumb tree,
like a speechless consolation
you turn into silence
every moment
the unbearable noise
that impatient man on this world makes.
I saw you as quietened forms and bowed down.
I saw that all pain is for ever being recovered
by the Terrible-Beautiful
and transformed into its *Bhairavi* melody
through a wordless song,
at the end of it all.

(Parisesh)

Seeing

Rows of thick black cloud
like a batch of tired wrestlers
came jostling in to rest in a corner of the sky
after the downpour of the night was over.

At the right end of the garden
a sudden ray of light descends
on the ripples made by waving *segun* tree blossoms
and the shadows in the wood are startled.

Vanaspati – A tree so large that it is imagined to be the lord of the trees.
Bhairavi – An Indian classical mode of a contemplative nature.
Segun – A big tree famous for the quality of its wood.

Sunshine in this month of *sravan*
has come like an unasked for guest,
causing mirth all around, in the trees, branches and leaves.

And stray thought warmed by sunlight
bgan to float in the far-away sky of my mind,
the day was gone, doing nothing.

In the afternoon come sudden thundery clouds
as if signalling someone's presence.
And in a moment heaps of clouds,
swollen in pride, leave their corner and rush on from all sides.
The water in the canal turns black,
darkness descends under the banyan tree.
And in the leaves of the distant wood
is announced the coming of the rain pouring forth.

In a moment the sky overcast by gathering rain becomes pale.
the meadow floods,
old trees like children shake around in disorder,
the palm leaves, the bamboo branches lose their pose.

Then it is all over.
Someone cleans up the sky.
The thin moon of the black fortnight
like a patient out of sickbed
appears in the courtyard with a tired smile.

My mind says: the scattered pieces of these little scenes
I do not want to be lost.
So many moements inthe stream of life
did once stand out in this raft of my seventy years,
often to disappear out of sight.
A few of these lazy days
I shall leave behind
in the leisured artistry
of fashioned language.
They will speak of this wonder,
one day I saw all this.   *(Punasca)*

Srawan – The fourth month of the Bengali year, it belongs to the rainy season.

51

Remembrance

A town in the West.
At one far and lonely corner
stands a neglected house
trying to keep out the heat of the day.
Its roof (in need of repair) overhangs on all sides.
Inside the rooms shadows lie prostrate
as if from eternity,
amidst an old smell
that is imprisoned there
for ever.

On the floor is a yellow coversheet
arond whose sides are printed
figures of tiger hunters with rifles.
In the north under the *sishu* tree
runs a mud road, where the dust is blowing
like a light shawl wrapped round bright sunlight.

Yonder in the sandy land
rising above the bed of the river
are fields of lentils and melons.
Further away glistens the river Ganges.
On it, here and there, are boats, pulled to the bank with ropes
looking like a picture drawn in ink.

On the verandah the grain parcher
– silver bangles on her forearms –
is grinding wheat between stones
singing a monotonous tune.

Girdheri, the doorkeeper, is sitting by her side
a long time
who knows with what excuse.

Sishu – A big tree.

Under the mangosa tree
is the well.
From it the gardener is drawing water
with the help of a cow.
The afternoon is pained
by the screeching noise that this makes.
But the cornfield is stirred
with the water flowing through.

The hot wind carries the faint smell of mango blossoms
while it brings the news that the bees have gathered
– as in a fair –
on mangosa sprouts.
In the afternoon a woman from another land comes from the town,
her face is thin, pale, sad.
She continues with the teaching of poetry from some foreign poet,
in a soft voice.
In the indistinct light with which mingles
the shadow of the blue hanging door screen,
amidst the smell of wet *khuskhus*,
enters some pain of the human heart, from beyond the sea.

The youth of my past keeps on looking for its own expression
in this foreign tongue,
just as the butterfly flies around
amidst the well-laid flower beds
of foreign season flowers,
with their multitude of colours.

(Punasca)

Khuskhus – A kind of scented grass. A wet curtain made of khuskhus is hung at the
door or a window to cool the room during summer.

The World of the Insect

On this side, on the branch of the *kamini* tree
the spider has let hang a fringe, as if made of dew.
On the other, in the garden by the roadside
is the anthill, with specks of red dust
scattered around.

I pass through, between the two, morning and evening,
preoccupied, I notice the sprout in the *sewli* tree
and the flowers that have bloomed covering the *tagar*.

In this vast universe the tiny household of man
appears small, but we know it is not so.
Nor is indeed the world of insects.
We do not quite see how,
but they too exist in the centre of creation.
They have a long history,
many things to fight through, many problems, many needs
running through aeons.
Through them, day after day, night after night,
spreads the invincible eager march
of the force that is life.
I pass through their midst,
but hear no sound that comes
from the long flow of their sentience
bearing hunger and thirst, life and death.

I hum a tune of half a song
think around the other half
that with it will well match.
This search, strange, happening for no reason,
has no meaning
in the universe of the spider
or the society of ants.

Kamini – A middle-sized flower bush with white scented flowers.
Sewli – White scented flower on orange stalk, blooms at the end of the rainy season.
Tagar – Unscented white flower.

But in their silent world
is there not already
a melody in each touch,
a song in each smell,
an unheard conversation in each mouth,
in each movement an unexpressed pain?

I am human;
I know I have an entry into the whole world,
into distant planets, stars, comets.
My doors open as obstacles move.
But the world of the spider
remained closed to me for ever.
For ever the curtain screening that ant's heart
remained drawn for me,
Right beside my life,
troubled with joys and sorrows.
I tread the path that runs
outside the bounds of their tiny universe,
morning and evening;
and I see the buds on the *sewli* tree,
the abundance of flowers on the *tagar*.

(Punasca)

An Ordinary Woman

I am a woman who stays at home,
you would not know me,
your last novel, Saratbabu
"a garland of withered flowers", I did read.
Your heroine Elokeshi was seized by death's fangs
at the age of thirty-five,
she also found herself in a state of war
with the age of twenty-five.
I see that you are noble enough
to let her come out a winner.

Let me tell you something of myself.
I was then rather young,
someone was touched by the grace
of that green age.
That knowledge used to send
a thrill through my body.
I forgot, I am rather ordinary.
There are thousands and thousands of women, very much like me,
those who have only the magic of youthfulness
to show for their youth.

I beg of you
write a story about an ordinary woman.
She is long-suffering.
If within the depth of her nature
something uncommon does lie buried
how would she prove it?,
how many are there, who could even come to know it?
Most people's eyes are open only to the magic of age,
their minds do not thirst for truth.
So are we sold out
for the price of chimeras.

Let me tell you what prompted all this.
Suppose that his name is Naresh,
who once said, 'I have never set my eyes on anyone
quite like you'.
I did not have the courage to believe
something so enormous –
nor the strength to disbelieve.

One day he went away to England,
a letter came only occasionally.
I thought, 'for shame, are there all that many women there
and do they all struggle to crowd in around him.
Are they all very extraordinary,
frightfully intelligent, bright?
Have they all discovered one Naresh Sen,
whose existence at home lay hidden
amongst the multitude?

The final letter said that he went sea-bathing with Lizzi,
quoting a few lines from Bengali poet:
you know, where *Urbasi* (the heavenly nymph) rises from the sea.
They sat afterwards side by side
on the sand.
In front undulated the waves of the blue sea,
the sky was full of clear sunlight.
Lizzi had said, softly, 'You came only the other
day and will soon be gone.
The two shells of the cockle,
let the middle be full
with one solid drop of tear,
priceless, rare!'
What an extraordinary style of speech!

Naresh adds, 'If these words are just made-up,
what does it matter?
They are charming, all the same'.
You may say, 'a golden flower set with diamonds,
is it real?
but is it not!?'

Urbasi – A mythical being. Name of a celestial nymph who was famous for her
everlasting youth and beauty.

57

You can well understand, the hint in his letter
of this comparison, like an unseen thorn,
pricks me near my heart,
it says, I am indeed very ordinary.
I have no such wealth
as can pay for that which is priceless.
All right! Let it be.
Let me be in debt for my entire life.

I appeal to you.
Write a story, Saratbabu,
of a very, very ordinary woman;
miserable, she has to compete from a distance
with five or seven extraordinary ladies
–struck at once with arrows from seven illustrious warriors*
(in this case female).
I understand, my fate is sealed.
So, I acknowledge defeat.
But she of whom you would write
let her win out, on my behalf.
My bosom will swell with pride as I read about her.
And I say, let there be a blessing on your pen
with flowers and incense.

Let her be called Malati,
that happens to be my name.
Have no fear, no one will know
there are many a Malati in Bengal
they know neither German nor French.
What they know is the language of tears.

How will you make her win?
You are high-minded, your pen full of noble sentiments.
You will probably take her on the path of sacrifice
to the limit of suffering, like *Sakuntala.*

---

*Arrows from seven illustrious warriors is an allusion to a Mahabharata story.
Abhimanyu, a son of Arjuna, was virtually unconquerable as an archer by a single
combatant. He was enticed by the Kauravas, the enemies, to enter into a certain
battle formation where he was struck down by arrows shot simultaneously by seven
illustrious warriors.

Have pity,
come down to my level.
The impossible boon that I beg of the gods
in the dark of night in bed
I shall no doubt not get.

But let your heroine receive.
Why don't you keep Naresh in England for seven years.
Let him fail in his exam, every time,
living in idleness amongst the circle of his admirers.
Let Malati in the meantime
pass her M.A.
from the Calcutta University.
With one stroke of your pen
you can make her come out first in Mathematics.
But if you stop there,
there will be a stain on your name
as a great novelist.
Whatever may be my situation,
let that not curb your imagination.
You are not as niggardly as God.

Send the girl to Europe.
There those who are wise, learned, of heroic stature,
poets, artists, men of royal lineage,
let them flock around her from every side.
Like astronomers, let them make a discovery of her
not just as someone erudite, but as a woman.
The magic that is in her, world-conquering,
let that be revealed, not in the country of dullards
but amongst the connoisseurs, those who know how to appreciate
in the lands where live the English, the German, the French.

Why not have a meeting called to honour Malati,
a meeting of the most distinguished.

Sakuntala – The name of the heroine of the famous Sanskrit drama *Shakuntala* written by Kalidas, daughter of a sage and a celestrial nymph and abandoned by her mother immediately after her birth. She was brought up by another sage in an ashram and she suffered a great deal through her marriage to a king called Dushmanta.

Let us imagine there pour down words of flattery –
a torrent she weathers easily
like a sail-boat moving on waves.
They look at her eyes and whisper:
In her enchanting glance meet together
India's bright sunlight and raincloud.
'Let me tell you – on the side –
the grace of the creator has actually been bestowed on my eyes.
A pity I had to say it myself,
but I did not have the good luck
to meet a European connoisseur).
Then let Naresh appear in a corner
with his bevy of "extraordinary" women.

And after that?
After that the tale finishes,
the dream ends.
Alas, you ordinary woman,
of creator's energy
what a waste!

(Punasca)

Just a Man

A middle-aged man from the north
- his tongue Hindusthani
he is thin, tall.
His moustache is grey, his face, clean-shaven,
looks like a dried-up fruit.

He has a printed shirt on his body,
his *dhoti* is tucked tightly between his legs.
From his left shoulder hangs an umbrella,
his right hand clasps a small bamboo stick.
Feet sandalled, he is walking towards the town.
Rather misty sunlight is spreading through the cloud
on this morning of the month of *bhadra*.
Last night it was hot
and, as if covered up with a blanket,
it was panting.
This morning the mist-wet wind
is blowing, rather undecided, on the young branches
of the *amlaki* tree.

I saw the passer-by
at the limit of my universe,
where things move like insubstantial pictures.
I saw him as just a man.
He had no name, no designation, no pain
he was not in need of anything.
He was just a man
going towards the market
this *bhadra* morning.

He too saw me
at the outskirts of his world,

Dhoti - The Hindi version of Bengali 'dhuti', a white garment for men.
Amlaki - A middle-sized tree that loses its leaves. Its fruit is used for
  Ayurvedic medicine.
Bhadra - The Fifth month of the Bengali year, beginning of the season of sarat.

61

beyond which is waste land,
where in this blue mist
nobody has any relation
to anybody else,
where I too am just a man.

At home he has got a calf
a *moyna* bird in a cage.
His wife grinds wheat between stones,
on her wrist are thick bangles of brass.
He has a washerman for a neighbour;
a greengrocer for a shopkeeper;
He is also related by debt
to *Kabuli* moneylenders.
I am nowhere there in his world.
For him I am just a man.

(Punasca)

Moyna - A small talking bird, dark brown in colour.
Kabuli - An inhabitant of Kabul, Afganistan. Some of these people used to live in
   India and lend money at an exorbitant rate of interest.

The Santal Girl

The santal girl comes and goes
through a pebble-strewn path
under the *simul* tree.
Her slim black body is tightly wrapped
in a coarse sari.
Some absent-minded craftsman,
engaged by the creator
to produce a black-coloured bird
looked for his material in *sravan* cloud and lightning
and in its place
produced this woman.

Her invisible wings are hidden under,
the hint of flying mixes in her light tread.
In her immaculately shaped fore-arms
are a few white bangles of lac.
On her head a basket of earth
as she comes and goes.
The end of her sari,
waving a red line,
spreads the magic of *palas* in the sky.

This is the end
of the period of *paush*.
In the north wind one occasionally finds
the enchantment of the south.
On the *himijhuri* branches
slim, restless leaves glimmer
in this wintry sun.
In the pale blue sky the hawk flies at a great distance.

Simul- Silk-cotton tree. Flowers are big and of red colour with no scent. It blooms
    in spring.
Sravan - The time of the advanced rainy season.
Palas - A big flower tree with saffron coloured flowers that have no scent.
Paush - The ninth month of the Bengali year in the season of winter. Harvest time.
Himjhuri - Rabindranath gave his own names to various trees and flowers.
    Himjhuri is one of these names for a beautifully scented flower.

Under the *amlaki* tree,
where boys gather,
unripe fruits drop.
In the zigzag path through the wood
light and shade weave together.
Suddenly dry leaves whirl around
through the whim of the alerted wind.
Under cover of the bush
the chameleon with its neck swelled
sits quietly on the grass.
The santal girl comes and goes
with a basket on her head.

The construction has begun of my house,
to be made of mud.
The labourers are here.
Slowly they lay the foundation
with their backs to the sun.

Now and again
the whistle of a train
comes from a distance.
The periods of the day pass by, daytime moves to a close.
Bells ring out on the horizon
where it meets the sky.
I look on and think with some shame:
this is an adolescent girl.
In her body and mind
are blossoming
a woman's natural power of self-offering,
of nursing, in soft sweet care,

powers which are growing there
for some village household.
I have engaged these in labour.
in work that can be bought.
I thieve away that power
– to offer which a price
is a dishonour –
with money (a thief's instrument).
See, the santal girl comes,
her basket brimful with earth.   *(Bithika)*

Amlaki – A middle-sized tree that loses its leaves.

64

The Ill-fated

When I stand before you, fortune's unwanted,
my head automatically bends.
And I fear
as one fears stillness before destruction.
What a weight of sorrow.
How immense is your pain,
like benumbed, dense darkness,
covering your whole world, past and future.
The futility of your life,
unmeaning, stretches out measureless
like a burnt-out mountain
standing bare in the sun
with its naked heap of black rocks,
ugly and terrible.

At the end of all consolation, all paths meet
in the dark womb of dissolution.

*   *   *

If on the brink of nothingness,
you knock at the closed door
of life's burnt-out home,
who is there inside to respond?
You can hear the sigh of bewildered darkness,
see in the shattered world lying around
the enormity of broken-down hope.
To it one's head bows down
its temple towers rise high
towards the mountain
born of ultimate pain.

It seems that the Great Goddess of sadness
is engaged, in and through your life,
in an arduous penance.

65

Left behind,
she is binding in debt, her eternal beloved
through a great sacrifice of sorrow.
You are being made to turn aside from life –
there are a hundred excuses –
by a curtain in front drawn
by a demand for detachment.
On the other side
resides the world of space and time.

You sit still on the brink of limitless despair
speechless, as if banished from life.
And your eyes, tearless,
ask this question, again and again,
Why! Oh, why! *(Bithika)*

Fourteen

Amidst this black darkness
the last bird song is drowned.
The wind stands still,
leaves do not stir.
As if the stars this clear night
have come down
close to the silent mystery of the old mangosa tree
wrapped around by the drone of the cricket.

Then, suddenly, you held my hand tightly
and said, 'I shall never forget you'.
In the window, without a lamp,
my figure looked indistinct.
Under cover of that shadowy form
the diffidence that this innermost appeal of your heart
might have felt
was gone.

In that moment, your love, as if like heaven
spread around, to become eternal remembrance.
The sad joy of that moment
was like a tune played on time's *veena*
that extends to the far distant future, from birth to birth.
At that moment the real in me
found its own infinite being
in the depth of your feeling.
In that little message of your shaking voice
my life's searching found its own worth,
having received the undying.
Amidst the thousand things that constitute your world
I am there as somebody uniquely special,
somebody intensely alive.

Veena – A striking string instrument famous since ancient times. It has frets and
   two gourds are used in its construction, one at the top, the other at the bottom.

What lies beyond this moment
is of secondary importance.
Beyond it is death.
One day from this theatre of illuminated form
I shall turn aside.
To this world of joys and sorrows, now so immediately accessible,
the world of multiplicity of forms,
the shadows of my memory
will acknowledge their defeat.
The *krishnachura* tree that grows under your gate,
which your own hands water twice a day,
is too, becoming prominent,
will brush me aside,
outside the range of its leaves and branches
into the oblivion of this wide universe.
No matter,
even that is of secondary importance.

(Sesh Saptak – 14).

Krishnachura – A big flower tree. The flowers come in bunches of red and yellow.

Twenty-five

On this side of the wall
in flowery earthenware pots
plants are arranged in order.
On the border flowerbed
purple plants abound
neatly shaped with scissors.
On the body of the wall
are creepers, tied up.
They smile a sweet smile,
but you do not hear
any loud laughter.
They swing in the wind,
but there is no room
for any mad dancing,
bound as they are in the strict discipline
of the aristocrat.
To look at the garden it seems
it is like the harem of the *Mogul* emperors.
Adorned with royal care,
but guards are placed everywhere.
Everywhere spies keep an eye
on your behaviour.

On the other side of the wall
a tall eucalyptus
soars up straight.
On its side are two *sonajhuri* trees
voluble with an abundance of leaves.
Above their head is the blue sky
and its limitless expanse.

I have often looked at them
rather absent-minded.

Mogul- Name of the royal line established in India by the Muslim emperor
  Babar.
Sonajhuri - Name given by Rabindranath to a tree with yellow flowers.

Suddenly I became aware
of their soaring freedom.
I saw that the dignity of beauty
lies in its liberation.
These trees are outside caste, outside custom,
they are at east, natural.
Their order lies in the marrow of their bones
they have no need to be tied up
with rules that come from outside.
They swing their branches
in a long beat.
Bunches of their leaves come in many a design,
all through the wind spread their murmuring sound.

My mind woke up to what they suggest.
I said, 'I shall plant in the earth
this poetry from the tub,
I shall let their branches and leaves
scatter around
in a jungle
that rhythm, unlimited,
creates.'

(Sesh Saptak)

Twenty-nine

One day alone of long ago
somehow got tied down, bound,
through a song, a rhythm, a picture.
Time's messenger kept it aside
outside the pathway of everyday use.
In the immersion ceremony of ages
many a thing flew past the quay.
Somehow it got stuck at the bend,
Nobody knew.

In the wood of the month of *magh*
appeared mango buds,
quite a lot dropped.
In the month of *fulgun*
palas bloomed
covering up the earth underneath.
Between the sun of the month of *chaitra*
and the field where mustard grew,
between the meadow and the sky
there was a competition, as it were, between poets.

On the body of my day, the day which got stuck
no season, no brush
leaves any mark.
Once I lived in that day.
The day was easy going.
spread amongst many things,
things that crowded in, from sides, in front.
I had a glance at everything.
but had not seen it all.

Magh – The tenth month of the Bengali year, and the last part of winter.
Fulgun – The eleventh month, beginning of spring.
Palas – A big flower tree. The saffron coloured flowers bloom in spring, they have
   no scent.
Chaitra – Last month of the Bengali year, end of spring.

71

I had loved,
had not known
how much.
Much of it was waste.
Much was left over, absentminded,
in the cup of life's delight.

I had known that day in one garb.
Today I find its shape has changed.
All that was incoherent, indistinct
have disappeared.
Out of it something stands clear
something I see as if in a distant frame.
She is the newly married of the day.
Her body is slim,
the end of her grey sari is on her head
covering the bun.
I did not have then the opportune moment
to tell her all.
A lot that I said now and again
was really of not much consequence.
And then the time was gone.

Today I see her figure
standing still,
amidst the fence of light and shade.
It looks as if she wants to say something
but no – it does not happen.
I feel I want to turn back to stand by her side
– there is no way.

(Sesh Saptak – 29)

The Earth

Earth accept today my obeisance,
on the altar of day's end
closing in like the prostration of a last homage.

The fount of great vigour,
you are fit to be enjoyed by heroes.
In your nature is the contrast
of soft and hard,
the mixture of male and female,
you let swing man's life in insufferable contest.
Your right hand fills the cup with nectar,
your left shatters it to pieces;
and your playground resounds
to a loud laughter that mocks.
You make the hero's life very hard to obtain,
he who is heir to greatness.
The best you make costly,
you are pitiless towards those who ask for help.
In your trees and fields is hidden the struggle
that goes on at every moment,
the garland of its victory is won
in fruit and grain.
Your merciless battlefield extends everywhere
in land and water,
there the victory of life is proclaimed
only through the mount of death.
The tower of civilization's success
is raised on the foundation of your unconcern, pitiless,
where the slightest shortcoming
has to be paid for in full
in destruction's coin.

In the first chapter of your history
the might of the demon was invincible.
He was vulgar, barbaric, deluded.

73

His fingers were coarse,
devoid of beauty and skill.
With club and spear in hand
he caused havoc amidst mountain and ocean.
With fire and steam he churned
vile nightmares in the sky.
The sole ruler of the insentient world,
he was full of blind fury towards the living.

The gods arrived in the next era.
They sang chants for the taming of the demon.
The arrogance of non-life was conquered.
Her green carpet rolled down,
Earth took her seat, the nourisher of life.

On the summit of the eastern sky appeared dawn,
on the western sea-shore descended evening
with the pitcher of peace on her head.
The demon, tied in shackles, was subdued.
Yet, that primeval savage clings to your history.
Suddenly he creates chaos
in the midst of your planned order.
Suddenly he zigzags his way out
from the dark depths of your nature.
His madness remains mingled in your pulse.
The chant of the gods spreads night and day
through the sky, atmosphere and forest
in high, low and middle octaves.
Yet, from the underworld of your breast
the half-tamed serpent hisses out
from time to time.
Egged on by it, you hit out at your own offspring,
you reduce to ruin your own creation.
Today, I shall leave behind,
the homage of my battered, bruised life
at your kingdom established in good and evil
in honour of your glory,
bred in fearful, awe-inspiring beauty.

Under the dust of your earth
is concealed the hidden treasure

of noble life and noble death.
Today, I touch that treasure, I realise it
in my 'body and mind.
In that dust is stored the vanished bodies
of numberless men
of uncounted cycle of ages.
I too shall leave behind a handful of dust.
the end product of my joys and sorrows of a lifetime,
shall leave it in the midst
of this silent heap of sacred dust,
that swallows up all distinctions, all names, all forms.
Earth, bound in fixed barriers,
earth, soaring in the world of clouds,
earth, seated in meditation in the silence
of great mountain ranges,
earth, where the noise of the unceasing current
of blue waves resounds,
you are beautiful when full of food,
devoid of it, your look is terrible.
On the one side is your field of grain,
bent with the weight of ripening corn,
where the morning sun, content, daily wipes off the dew
with the veil of its rays,
and the setting sun leaves behind
in the rhythm of green corn
its unuttered message –
I am pleased.
On the other side is the desert
fruitless, parched and pale with terror.
There occurs the mirage of ghostly dance
amidst the skeletons strewn around.
In the month of *baisakh* I have seen
your storm advance like a black eagle
to snatch away the horizon
that is caught between the beaks of the lightning.

The the sky would roar like a lion, its mane
puffed up in anger.

Baisakh – The first month of the Bengali year, a part of the summer season when
frequent storms occur.

75

In the lashing of its tail would be upturned
the dispirited tree *Vanaspati*,
its branches scattered in disorder,
when the roof of a broken-down hut
would run away in the wind
like a prisoner released of his chain.
Again in the month of *falgun*, I had known
your soothing south wind to spread
mutterings of love and parting
through the scent of the mango blossom,
when from the cup of the moon
would overflow its rays
like the foam of some sacred beverage,
when the stormy wind would overreach the patience
of the murmuring forest
and make it break out in tumultuous noise.
You are soothingly peaceful and you are violent,
you are old and you are ever new,
you have emerged at the first dawn
that is past the age of counting,
out of the sacrificial fire of beginningless creation.
In the wheel of your pilgrimage
you have scattered the ruins
of many unfinished histories,
their meaning now lost.
You have left behind many discarded handiworks
stored in layers of oblivion
through countless time.
Nourisher of life, you have nurtured us
in small cages of segmented time
within which is the limit of our play,
the end of all our achievement.

I have not come before you today
with any delusion.
I shall not ask for immortality
for the garland I have threaded with the help of night and day
in long patience.

Vanaspati – Literally 'the lord of the forest'. A very big tree towering above others,
     like the fig or banyan, is referred to by this name.
Falgun – The eleventh month of the Bengali year, beginning of spring.

76

If out of great suffering
I have conquered and made fruitful a moment of my life,
if I have acknowledged the true value of one of the happenings
that occurs in a tiny segment of time,
flowing amongst the great moments that rise and sink
in the path of the sun's passage
over millions and billions of years,
then put a mark of your earth in my forehead,
the sign that will vanish
in that night,
when all signs merge back into the great unknown.

You, disinterested earth,
before you forget me completely,
on your pure, unstained feet
let me leave this, my obeisance.

(Patraput-3)

One day in the rainy month of *ashad*
descend dark shadows of black clouds pregnant with water
on the murmuring branches of the bamboo bush,
and the grain fields start to come alive
from plot to plot in slim sprouts of young rice plants.
This life is so abundant, so full, so vigorously joyous,
its signature spread wide and unhindered
in earth and atmosphere,
through light and air,
that it does not look as if
it can be contained
within the little fence we call 'time'.
In its soft, green expanse spread far and beyond,
the boundless ever calls,
as it does in the turbulent waves
of the ocean.

The month passes.
The affection that is *sravana* rain
pours down pretending to hurt
the green shoot that pushes ahead from day to day,
bearing the weight of seed pods
on its shoulder;
infinitely proud, as if in a victory march.
On its self-absorbed exuberance of youth
sunlight spreads its laughter and joy,
the night star fixes its gaze
in silent wonder.

The month passes.
The wild heavings in the wind stop.
From the quiet blue sky of the season of *sarat*

Ashad – The third month of the Bengali year, beginning of the rainy season.
Sravan – The fourth month of the advanced rainy season.
Sarat – The third season in the Bengali year, the time of the Bengali festival, Durgapuja.

a message comes in the deep sound of conch,
get ready.
The dew-bath rite is now completed and over.

The month passes.
The cruel wind of winter arrives from the Himalayas,
imprinting the suggestion of yellow onto the green.
Thus the colour of light replaces that of the earth.
A flock of geese fly over to the little island in the river,
bunches of *kasa* flower drop and settle along its bank.

The month passes.
The fields are emptied of the golden harvest,
reaped, it disappears
as if in some enclosure of darkness,
just as the end of the day
swallows up the afternoon sunlight
in the grey vanishing twilight.
In the empty fields
the signs of the past
remain for a time clinging to dead roots,
and are then burnt up in a flaming fire.

The month passes.
On the footpath through the meadow
the cowherd walks, herding his cattle.
This causes no pain, no loss to anyone.
In the field stands the lonely fig tree
enclosed in its own shadow –
like a sage meditating on the sun.
Under it, at noon, a boy plays on his flute
an ancient folk tune,
and the air under the copper-coloured hot sky
lets out a moan.

For it sounds like Time
pouring forth a sigh
that remains afloat on the ebb-tide of farewell
constantly taking place.
Time, the traveller, who cannot find
his way back to the left-behind inns
even for a day.   *(Patraput–4)*

Kasa – A kind of tall grass with flowers that feel like cotton.

79

Sleep is trying to take over my eyes
but from time to time I am aroused.
As the first shower of the rainy season, just arrived,
seeps through the earth to reach the root of trees,
so does this young *hemanta* sunlight
penetrate through sleep to the roots
of my unconscious being.
The time is about three o'clock.
Little patches of fine white cloud
are afloat, as if fixed, in the sunlight
of this month of *kartik*.
The look like paper boats,
let loose by the children of the gods.
The wind rushes forth from the west,
branches of the tamarind tree swing
hither and thither.
In the north lies the road
to the neighbourhood of the milkmen.
On it bullock carts raise up ochre dust
that spreads up to the light blue sky.
In this silent hour of the noon
my mind, on holiday from work, floats
in the raft of this unthinking day.
This day has come torn out of all purpose

that binds the world in a thousand strings.
This day is not tied down to any use.
Colourful, it will disappear in the evening
in the black sea of sleep's oblivion.

Notes-In Bengal there are six seasons, each consisting of two months, which
correspond, roughly to the following distribution of the months of the western
calendar: *grisma* (summer, April–May), *varsa* (rainy season, June–July), *Sharat*
(August–September), *hemanta* (October–November). (The end of this season has
some characteristics of early autumn. The Bengali month *Kartik* belongs to
this season), *shit* (winter, December–January), *vasanta* (Spring, February–
March).

In time's register this day will be written
only in faint ink,
soon to fade out of existence.
It will leave a gap amidst days
that are written down in deep letters
in the diary of men's fate.
The dry leaf from the tree falls on the earth,
it too pays back its debt.
This, my dropped leaf, my idle day,
has given nothing back to life.

Yet, my mind says:
surely to receive is also a way of giving.
The savour of delight that issues forth from sky to sky
in a thousand streams from the spring of creation,
I have received it in my body, in my mind.
Its hue has touched me with colour
as it has touched the rice field,
the green leaves in the wood,
the white veil of the run-away cloud
of *sarat*.
It is only through these
that today's picture of the world is complete.
A blaze of light flaired forth in my mind,
the warm breeze exhaled by *hemanta*
stirred me out of my state
of half-sleeping and half-awake
(like *ganga-jamuna* confluence).
All these too have assembled
in the frame,
wherein the total picture is depicted.
This pure delight of mine
which is shimmering through
the pleasure ground
of water, land and sky
with the restless leaves of the fig tree,
it will not be written down
as part of the history of this world.

ganga-jamuna – two famous rivers of India, considered to be sacred. The water of
   the Ganges is ochre coloured, that of Jamuna black. So this expression is used as
   a simile for the union of two opposite things.

But its flavour will nevertheless be there
amidst the manifold expressions
of this creation.
These moments which I, deeply immersed, savour as pure joy,
are like my heart turned into red lotus seeds
and which the seasons are threading a garland –
a garland gathered from the delight
of my whole life.
This lazy, undistinguished day
has left no gap,
it too has added a seed.

Last night I spent alone, by the side of this window.
On the forehead of the forest
was printed the shape
that the moon takes on the fifth day
of the clear fortnight.
This too is part of the same world.
But the artist changed the shape of the melody –
one that is sung
in the quivering of misty light.
The world that is busy
as it treads its way through the day
is now* like still life, relaxed,
the end of its sari spread in the courtyard.
It has no concern
for what is going on nearby
as it listens instead
to the ancient tales that are being murmured,
though the light given off by the stars –
reminding it of its
gaseous childhood
of remote past.
The trees stand as if dumb-struck,
their bodies made of concentrated silence
of the night.
In the faintly visible green of the grass
their shadows are reflected in a row.

*It is possible to speak of last night in the present tense, in Bengali.

During the day
these shadows were
like serving maids
standing to the side
of the running business that is life.
They have given shelter to the cowherd,
a rest from the intense sun.
Now with nothing to be busy about
in this moonlit night
they sit
resting on the body of this night light.
Like small brothers and sisters together
they have used their brush
in a composition
that seems a whimsical task.
My day time mind
changed the key of its sitar.
I reached as if some neighbour of this earth
that one can see through a telescope.
The feeling which stirred deep in my heart,
I spread widely in the very heart of creation.
The moon, the stars, these dark trees
came together as one, like omnipresence
and reached fullness of being
in my knowing.
That the world has found me,
has found itself in my consciousness,
this is what gives worth
to the life of the idle poet.

(Patraput – 7)

Someone brought me this wild seedling,
its leaves are yellowy green
its flowers purple, like cups with artistry made
to drink sunlight out of.
I ask, 'what is it called?'
No one knows.
It inhabits that infinite domain
where belongs the unknown
among the nameless stars of the heavens.
I have brought it down with a name
with which to call it
in the privacy of my familiarity
I share with nobody.
The name, Peyali.

The garden sent an invitation around.
It ws taken up by dahlia, fuschia, marigold.
This one lived uncared-for,
in the total autonomy of non-identification,
outside caste.
This one is a *Baul*, this one is not social.
Before long it happened,
the flower, dried up, dropped.
The amount of flutter that this caused in the air
is too faint to hear.
The minutes which together
spanned the zodiac in its horoscope
add up to a sum that is infinitesimal.
The honey contained in the depth of its bosom
measured no more than a drop.

Baul – A distinctive religious community that exists outside orthodoxy and both
    Hindus and Muslins can belong to it. It is famous for its direct approach to God.
    who is believed to be found in the heart of man also for its songs which are used as
    substitutes for ritual. Bauls are tree beings who roam about preaching love of
    God through singing.

This one completes its journey in a tiny fraction of time
as does the luminous sun
– a flower with fire for its petals –
in an aeon.
Its history is written on the corner of a tiny page
with a tiny pen
by the creator-chronicler.

Yet, alongside its existence
unfolds history that is so vast
that you can hardly finish a page
to go on to the next.
The unceasing flow of centuries
is like a wave whose rhythm is a slow beat.
In its current rise mountains,
deserts and oceans change their dress.
This little flower's primal resolve to be
has come forward to join in this outstretched flow
of endless time,
shaped by the continuous force and counterforce
of creation.
Along this path where flowers bloom to drop
through millions and billions of years
that old resolve to be continues anew;
it stays fresh, for ever active.
No one has yet seen
what its completed picture would look like.
I muse on that unseen
in whose meditation is held
ever present
this resolve unembodied, this picture not drawn in line,
the unseen in the limitless imagination of which
I exist,
wherein is held the whole history of men,
past and yet to come.

(Patraput – 8)

I sit at the ferry station
on the bank of an afternoon,
close to the last step,
my feet submerged under the water
as it flows, dark and silent.
The field of life's forsaken festivity
lies behind, with its accumulation of left-overs
from many years.
A thought occurs –
there has been many a gap
time and again
in life's big build-up for pleasure.
So often when I could afford to pay
the market had still to get going.
When at last the boat, full of merchandise
came to port,
the gong had already been struck.
The hour to buy and sell was over.
Once came an untimely spring
arousing the cuckoo at dawn.
That day I fixed strings to my sitar
and a tune to my song.
Someone was to hear it,
but when her hair was at last dressed,
a saffron-coloured sari on her bosom properly placed,
came the hour of light and shade.
My *Multan raga* melody had then turned sad in weariness.
Soon the grey light was swallowed up in a black smudge.
My interrupted song sank –
like a little raft afloat with a burnt-out lamp –
maybe in the recesses of someone's mind.
Perhaps it gave rise to a sigh,
but no light was lit.

Multan Raga – Raga is the name for certain classical musical modes. Multan is an
ara of Indian Punjab. A classical raga which is influenced by the folk tradition
of Multan is called 'Multan Raga'.

For this I complain no more.
The dark cave of loneliness
had, out of its starved abyss, day and night
poured forth a stream of stirred melody.
In its veil, as it danced all day, played
the seven colours of sunlight.
In its dark, dense, noisy current
found release the rhythm
that occurs at depth of night
in a rapt meditation chant.
And the emptiness of my burning midday
has flowed into the slow expanse
of prologue to the raga "Gour-sarang".
Today I say that life, however deprived,
is worthwhile.
Its store of suffering is being emptied,
offered as a homage to death.
And at one corner of the altar that is time's
will forever remain
its gift of payment due.

Man takes his journey on the path of life
to discover himself.
I have caught in my heart the man who sings,
the man who brings life I have missed.
All that I have known is my own secluded form
hemmed in by shadows –
like a lake without current in a valley.
There, from the trees at the bank
flowers drop at the end of spring.
Children play with toy boats.

Women fill up their pitchers
amidst gurgling noise and foaming bubbles.
In its bosom, the rains, fresh
and wrapped in green, in sublime magnificence,
find a sportive companion.
When the Nor'wester suddenly beats its wing,
the still water goes through a turbulence of unease,

Gour-sarang – Name for a classical musical mode, one of the fundamental ones.

and impatience is stirred up
in its embanked immobility.
Then it seems as if
a mad waterfall rushing down from the mountain top
has turned itself
into the dumb lake at the foothills,
and being bound has forgotten
its own passionate wildness,
that once welled up.
It did not jump over stones,
smashing down its own boundaries.
It did not challenge the unknown at every turn
thundering its message, so long suppressed;
nor did it create whirlpools
to scatter around its hidden depths.
I have not known in myself
the terrifying, mighty man.
who rescues life by force
from the fangs of death.
I, feeble, pale,
am making my exit
in the dishonour of
not having been expressed.

On the other side of terror, difficult to tread,
awaits the goddess of wisdom, in darkness.
The prisonhouse of man, sky-reaching
has turned its arrogant aspires, bound in black stones
towards sunrise.
On its door is painted
folded palms, sad, wounded,
of many centuries,
and the trace of rebellion, blood-stained.
The best treasure of the god of history
lies hidden in the iron-fort of demons.
In the sky is head a voice
the general of the gods calls –
'come ye, those who would conquer death'.
The trumpet was sounded,
yet, no battle thirst
was stirred in my secure life of apathy.

I have not forced open its formation
to take my place amidst the war efforts
of battling gods.
I have only heard in dreams the
thump of kettle drums,
only the footfalls of marching soldiers
have entered my heart from the outside
to mingle with its throbs.
The ray of familiarity
with that fearful man, death-draped,
who creates life anew,
age after age,
amidst the deluge of destruction
has remained dimmed in my existence
All I leave behind is an obeisance,
a bowed-down head
at the feet of that hero
enshrined in men's hearts,
who creates paradise on earth
at the cost of death –
through suffering
that illumines.

(Patraput – 12)

A Dream

A dense dark night
the wind of the rainy season
is beating in a gust on all sides.
The clouds thunder in a deep heavy voice,
the doors shake,
now and again the windows grate.
I look outside
at the rows of betel nut and coconut trees.
They shake their head in impatience.
Amongst the dense branches of the jackfruit tree
lumps of darkness oscillate
like some combination of ghosts.
From the road falls a streak of light
on one corner of the pond,
zigzag, like a serpent.

I remember these lyrical lines:
'a dense dark *sravan* night, grave is the sound of thunder clouds
I dreamt a dream at that time'.
Behind the picture of *Radhika*
there was some woman –
a model for the poet –
in whose heart was sprouting the bud of love.
She was rather shy –
there was collyrium in her eyes –
she came back from the bathing pond
wringing her wet blue sari.

This stormy night
I want to bring to my mind
through a picture of her morning and her evening,

Sravan night– Sravan is the fourth month of the Bengali year and the last half of the
  rainy season. The expression 'sravan night' suggests the mood of love that occurs
  during the downpour.
Radhika– The famous lady-love of Krishna of the Puranas (religious literature).
  She is used as the symbol for the pure love of God.

her words and thoughts,
her glance,
the Bengali woman the poet knew
three hundred years back.
It is not distinct.
She is wiped out behind the shadow of the women of today,
the way they bring the end of their sari
round their shoulder,
the way their bun is made up, twisted around,
set slightly low down,
the way they look at you with (no-nonsense)
straightforward eyes,
this was not the picture the poet had
three hundred years back
Yet, 'dense, dark *sravan* night...
I dreamt a dream at that time'.
In a *sravan* night of that time
the wind of the rainy season had blown in gusts
the same way as today.
There is then something common
between dreams of today
and those of days past.

(Shyamali)

91

The Savour of Life

Let me hear,
I am lending my ear.
The day is coming to a close.
The birds are singing their last song,
the song to exhaust all the resources of their throat,
at the day's end.
They have drawn me, mind and body
into the sanctuary of their being,
of many a tune, many a colour,
many a play.
Their history does not have much to say,
except this, 'we are here, we are alive,
alive at this fantastic moment'.
Only this, but it has reached me
in the very centre of my being.
Women dip their pitchers to fill with water,
I too have plunged my mind to fill myself
with this murmur of life
from the sky.

Give me some time.
I am lending my mind.
The daytime is ebbing away.
In this afternoon light, spread all over the grass,
happens the pleasure of the trees,
a pleasure that is hidden in their depth,
is scattered in their leaves.

My breath has spread itself in the wind.
It receives the touch, the savour
of life that is the universe,
the savour that comes filtered through my consciousness.
Let me sit on
with my eyes open.

You have come to argue.
Today I have a little time, at this day's end,
amidst the declining sunlight.
There is nothing good about it or bad,
nothing to blame or praise
nothing to fight about or doubt.
But there is the green of the forest.
the sparkle of water,
and on the upper storey of my life
a little tremble, some confused noise,
a ripple.
This little leisure of mine
is flying like a short-lived insect
to finish off the last play of its coloured wings
in the sunset sky.

Pose no unnecessary question,
the demands you are making are useless.
I am sitting on the other side of the present,
a sloping bank that inclines to the past.
My life, chased around by many a pain,
has once played amidst light and shade,
that branches of trees along the row
in a grove, interweave.

It is now noon in the month of *asvin*,
Amidst the trembling grass,
the meadow, the *kasa* grove,
the soliloquy that floats about in the wind
has mingled with the gaps
which exist in the *veena* that is my life.
Many problems like a net
bind the world with a thousand strings from all sides.
For me their knots have disappeared.
The travellers on their last journey
have left behind no preparation, no anxiety,
no longing.

Asvin - The sixth month of the Bengali year, latter half of the season of sarat.
Kasa - A kind of grass with flowers that feel like cotton.
Veena - A string instrument with frets used since ancient times.

This message only remains
in the tremble of the leaves –
they too lived,
this is truer than the fact
that they are no more.
Today we can only sense
some hint of the colour of their garment,
of the wind that was stirred up as they passed by,
hint of the message that they looked and saw,
·of the rhythm of their love –
the current of life from the west – like the river *Jamuna*
amidst the eastern flow – like the river *Ganga*.

(Shyamali)

Jamuna – A river famous for its associations with Krishna.
Ganga – The most famous river in India revered by Hindus as sacred.

The Eternal Traveller

They have emerged in great crowds out of the dim past,
they are seekers, devotees of truth.
They have come out through the lion gate of ancient time
the shape of whose tower
scratches lines in the unknown script
of a lost language.

They are pilgrims, warriors.
They march on forever towards the future.
The battle goes on,
the trumpet of all times resounds.
The earth shakes
to the sound of footfalls of many hundreds of ages.

When the night is half gone the heart throbs,
the mind feels detached.
Money and honour seem useless,
death becomes dear.
Those who had vigour in their bones,
those who took to the road
are travelling even today, beyond death.
Those who clung to their shelter,
half-dead in life,
their motionless homes
are now on the sandbank of the dumb sea.
In their worldwide ghostly land
amidst impure air
who will build a home,
who will turn a blind eye
and heap up
useless stuff?

At the beginning of time man stood
on the crossroads of this universe.
His travelling expense lay in his blood, it lay in his dream,
he found it on the road itself.

As soon as he made a design
and built a house of bricks
– its roof almost touched the clouds –
the foundation began to give way
under the earth, worm-eaten.

* * *

Sometimes he had fallen asleep
amidst a flagging gathering of drunken orgy, in a dark corridor,
sitting in a sofa of comfort.
Then from the dark undergrowth
leapt some headless nightmare
like a mad animal;
with a groaning noise
it tried to tear asunder his throat.
The ribs of his breast shook with a rapping noise
and he awoke amidst a feeling of suppressed suffering –
like the pain of death.
Mad with grief he had smashed his wine cup,
had torn off the flower garland,
then rushed out on a difficult path, blood stained,
beyond the century, punctured with a thousand holes,
towards an unknown, unseen destination,
with each pressure of the blood on his heart
the tabor had sounded a grave, serious note:
go beyond, go beyond.

Oh, eternal traveller,
care not for name,
hope not for accomplishments,
oh, child of man, turned-out-of-door.
From ages past
are advancing those who would break all barriers;
leaping over fences, pounding stones in a smooth passage,
crossing mountains.
In the sky the eternal trumpet calls
'stop not, move on, go beyond'.

(Shyamali)

A Sudden Meeting

Suddenly I met her in a railway compartment,
I never believed it was possible.

I had often seen her
in a sari that was red,
like the colour of pomegranate.
Today she was clad in a black silk garment
that went over her head,
and round her slim, fair face –
fair like the *dolonchapa* flower.
It seems that through this black colour
she has created a secret distance around her,
a distance that goes right to the limit of the mustard field
to end at the bluish haze of the *sal* forest.
I was taken aback
to find a fimilar person
shrouded by the gravity of unfamiliarity.

Suddenly she dropped back the newspaper
and folded her palms at me.
So the doors opened to the usual civilities,
I started the greeting:
'how are you, how is your family'
and so on.
She kept looking outside, through the window
as if her glance was not meant to be touched
by anything close at hand.
She answered one or two questions,
some she ignored.
The gestures of her hand said
it was futile to indulge in all this talk,
far better just to remain quiet.

Dolonchapa– White flower with a sweet scent, it resembles the lily.
Sal– A prominent, big tree of West Bengal.

I was on a different bench,
at a distance,
among her companions.
Her fingers signalled, come closer.
So I came to sit beside her.
I thought this act of her was rather courageous.
Sheltering behind the noise of the train,
softly, she said,
'Please do not mind.
We have not much time to waste
I must get off at the next station.
You are going far
and we shall never meet again.
I want to hear from your own mouth
the answer to the question
that has remained in suspense
all this time.
Will you give a true answer?'

I said, 'I will'.
She continued looking outside, at the sky,
and asked,
'those days of ours,
the days past,
are they really over, altogether,
is nothing left at all?'

I remained silent for a moment,
then said,
'All the stars of the night
exist in the depth of daylight'.
Then misgiving came,
'have I just made it up?'
She said, 'this is enough,
now you may go away, to the other side.'
At the next station everyone got off.
I continued travelling, alone.

(Shyamali)

8

When the lamps were blown out one by one
from the stage, the theatre emptied, the realm
of vast silence pointed its finger at me. At that
peace came to my heart like deep sleep,
wherefrom even dreams have been cleaned
out – plastered in inky darkness.
The dress that I had put on, from the first
opening up of the curtain for so long,
to tell the people of my role, was no longer needed.
I had marked myself with many signs, decked myself
up with many colours, to please the multitude;
the value of these was wiped out. Wonder-struck,
I found the deepest fulfilment of my being
in my own self; as the clear sky is dumb
with speechless surprise to confront
its own star-studded form, when at the last rite
of sunset the many splendoured lines and colours
of this earth get lost
in the emptiness of the day's end.

(Prantik)

A Woman on a Pilgrimage

She is on a pilgrimage, with effort managing
to cover the last half a mile of the journey of her life.
In her hand a bag of beads,
a bundle on her side,
she is sitting patiently in a station since the dawn.
Half-formed thoughts cross her mind:
'perhaps there is some other station somewhere else,
where fruitlessness
receives back in itself
all lost offerings in fresh significance,
where shadows find form, taking shape in embodiment.'
In her bosom are stirred
a thousand voices of a left-behind past,
familiar since childhood.
And at the end of her days
the frustrated hopes of a neglected life
are out to find a home
in some distance land unknown.

The day she started on her journey
the sky smiled at her
in fresh sunlight.
Today, where she finds herself,
the strangers around and their unfamiliar voice
appear as so much meaningless noise.

Once, on the way, she offered her beloved
her youth –
a flavour of honeyed intoxication,
not unmixed with pain,
that gave her both joy and sorrow.
The empty cup of that offering today shows neglect,
like a tired autumn afternoon
unmixed by the bee buzzing around.

Today, those who are journeying on
to seek a companion
leave her on a side.
With her withered, shaking hands
she will no longer be able to light a lamp
for someone,
who is looking for a fellow-traveller
on a difficult path
in a night of stormy weather.

*　　*　　*

Left behind, alone, she thinks may be she will
find at some far away place something
invaluable, heavenly, beyond all taints of the mundane.
Alas, this something will travel before her
like a ghost, and in fading light she will follow,
hoping everyday to get hold
until in the dark it finally disappears.

(Sejuti)

Half-past Nine

The clock says it is half-past nine.
In the morning cold, rather mild,
the wind is, as it were, sunbathing in drowsiness,
in the valley under the hill
at the top of the wood,
on the inviting green of the leaves.
The radio plays in the living room
filling the atmosphere with a flood of melody
from beyond the sea.
A foreign lady sings in a foreign tongue,
a distance of thousands of miles conceals her
in which everything that she is, is submerged
but for rhythm and tune.
The touch of this music, bodiless without a surrounding,
is being dissolved
through my consciousness.
The period of the day flowing along which
this voice has come
is outside the time thread of this land.
Alone, bearing the lamp of a musical mode,
she is approaching
as if like a lover to an assignation,
all buden cast off.
The obstacle of mountains, rivers, oceans,
she has not heeded.
She has made her way through
the confused noise of many a language,
treading along life and death, ceremony and grief.
The cruel killings of battle fields
the trifling gossip of many millions of homes
have left her alone, shying, as if, from all contact.
Not a part of this world,
she is only a musical current, detached.
The song of the parted *Yaksha*, '*Meghdut*',

Meghdut-A poetic composition by the great Sanskrit poet Kalidas. It describes the
pain of Yaksha (a mythical being, who sends his love to his beloved, from whom
he is forcibly separated for a year) through the verses of this book.

102

that too is queer like this, I think.
The name only is there, not the poet,
who is nowhere to be seen.
By its side are silent,
the numberless faces of the world of that day.
On it no light has fallen,
from *Ujjayini*, that was bright,
bubbling with life
on a morning of that age.
Its rhythm renders futile
even a king's might.
It has travelled over
many ages that are now past,
along the revolution of time,
of which it carries no sign.
The volubility of this immense universe
is made motionless on the canvas
of its couplets.

(Nabajatak)

Ujjayini - A town in ancient India said to be the capital of King Vikramaditya, identified with a town of the Middle Provinces of modern India.

The Turning away of the Mind

Her mind is like a river
suddenly flooded,
that turns round to an unthought of path
drawn by who knows what.
That is its natural flow
however much this turning away may harm
the ripening corn,
you may wish to bind it on its regular course,
but when the rains come the river with its strong current
will again and again burst its bank
and you will find yourself wrong.
She is not a plaything, nor a pet to caress,
let your mind understand this message.
In the force of some current
her frothy laughter, uncontrollable,
anytime will make itself known.
You may sail your frail craft
wherein your heart's merchandise is gathered.
All of a sudden she will mock your effort
and smash it all as if against a stone.
So disaster will strike your play
through her negligence.
If you know this just as playfulness
know how to mix your laughter with hers
you will have nothing to repent.
To want to sail as if on a tide
along the path that the spring takes,
that is death like insistence.
You say she is free
but that is a mistake.
She is no more free
than the comet is,
which drops suddenly,
awakening, as it were, from sleep,
through the sheer fault of its fate.
Learn how not to take umbrage.

If it is with flood that you wish to play,
you have to keep out all thought of gain.
If you are a dealer of things
have nothing to do with the mountain stream.
That which has a price of any kind
should be kept confined
at home with care,
and not be invested in a business
that insists on mad movement.
Swim only if you have to,
know how not to sink in slime in a whirlpool.
If you do not know how to keep yourself afloat
on the bank of hope,
then know this to be the only safe course
however full of boredom.
She is mine, this pride is in vain
for the imprint of mockery will be on your forehead.
In detached play there is no demand for giving or getting,
only coming and going from a distance –
for the human heart is a mysterious flame.

(Sanai)

The Wrong Time

It is afternoon, the harvest is over,
the field is empty of corn.
The niggardly earth is exuding heat
in the month of *baisakh*.
I do not know how, through some mistake,
leaving its wood habitat,
to this grey poverty and dry dust,
the *bulbuli* bird has come.

Bearing the memory of the morning
in its own heart
it is searching for the abundant hospitality
that the younger earth once offered,
through her fullness that was seen
in crimson and green.
Would it have to go back in the dark,
thinging 'it must be an illusion, all that'?

Yet, it sang
and made a gift of that without return.
What did it have to tell, amidst this doubt,
to whom did it aim?
That which is seemingly gone,
still remains, taking another form.
Maybe the bird understood this truth,
in its own thought.

The wealth of the morning,
of which not a speck remains
did happen. This consolation never dies.
The truth that we receive only for a moment
does not with the moment die.
The morning bird in its evening song
brings precisely this message of joy.   *(Sanai)*

Baisakh – The first month of the Bengali year, season, summer.
Bulbuli – A small, black singing bird, rather like the thrush.

106

4

Once you gave me
as a loan to my eyes
unlimited daylight.
Now, my king, you are staking your claim
to take that back.
I am aware I have to let go of what I owe,
you still announce your shadow
through the evening lamp.
I came only as a guest
to this creation you have fashioned
with your light.
If here and there are left unclaimed
a few pieces, incomplete,
in some tiny unnoticed gaps,
let them be,
leave them alone uncared for,
where your chariot
leaves its last mark
in the finality of dust.
There, let me build my world
amidst a little light,
a little shadow –
some illusion.
Chasing after light that is vanishing in the path of shadow,
it may pick up something –
the tiniest fragment that is left
when my debt to you is paid.

(Rogsajyay)
(in sickbed)

107

5

In this infinite universe
the wheels of suffering ply,
grinding down planets and stars;
the scattered sparks
fly around with great passion
in all directions
to wrap the sad pain of existence
in the dust-web of sorrow
wrought by destruction.
In the machine room of torture
amidst glowing consciousness,
somewhere is heard the clanging noise of spears and shells,
somewhere blood from a scar is oozing out.
This tiny body of man,
how immense is its power to bear torture!
In this assembly of creation and destruction,
man has to drink life out of a chalice of fire.
Why, but for the fierce madness of the creator,
did he have to join
in this *bhairavi* wheel of life,
why otherwise must tears flood
the blood-red lamentation
that fills his body's earthen vessel?
Yet, to all this
man's unconquerable consciousness
has given an uncountable value.
The offering that he has poured
in the *homa*-fire of his body's pain
in an ascetic self-conquering attempt
to reach the stars,
has no equal anywhere.
Such wealth of unconquered vigour,
such fearless patience;

Bhairavi – A Tantric symbol for the play of ultimate energy through the union of
 opposites.
Homa – A Vedic sacrifice offered to various gods through the intermediary of fire.

such refusal to be cowed down by death,
such a victory march,
in search of the very limit of suffering
by group after group of men
who walk on treading over beds of fire! What is that nameless,
flaming pilgrimage
for which man has such
inexhaustible travelling expense in the form of love,
such source of self-giving
that forces itself out of the womb of fiery volcanoes
to walk with him on his path?

(Rogsajyay)
(in sickbed)

Dark night, ancient out of all reckoning!
Today amidst this black confusion of disease
I see you in my mind's eye,
at the very beginning of existence –
seated in a meditative pose
in contemplation of creation.
Your loneliness is fearsome,
You are dumb, blind.
I saw in the endlessness of spheres
the same effort for bringing something forth,
that goes on in this diseased, tired body of mine.
There, existence, as yet crippled,
is crying out of the bottomlessness of sleep,
as hunger for self-expression
flashes out in flames, in secret,
from the molten womb of iron.
Unconscious, your fingers
weave the image of an indistinct art work.
And from the depths of the primeval ocean
suddenly swell up lumps of existence
like huge dreams
deformed, incomplete.
They are waiting in darkness
to achieve fullness of being
in time's gracious right hand,
where the uncouth, the ugly, will find a well-balanced body,
in the freshness of sunlight.
The image-maker will then chant his incantations
and there slowly will unfold
the creator's hidden resolve.

(Rogsajyay No. 9)

I wake up in the morning
and find in the vase,
a rose.

A question recurs to my mind –
the energy that has brought it
out of the revolution of time
to this beautiful end,
escaping all blackage of the ugly, the incomplete,
at every step,
is that blind, absentminded,
like a *yogi* seeking renunciation,
who makes no distinction
between the ugly and the beautiful –
energy that seeks knowledge, seeks action,
but has no truck with emotion?
People argue
that in the assembly of creation
the ugly and the beautiful have equal recognition,
there exists no guard to bar either of them
from entrance.
I, a poet, know no argument.
I see this universe in its wholeness,
see millions and billions of stars and planets
in the spheres,
that carry grace and grandeur,
the rhythm of which is unbroken, melody unhindered,
where no false step creates the deformed;
and I see in the sky
a grand shining rose
where its millions of petals unfold.

(Rogsajyay No. 21)

Yogi – A practitioner of spiritual discpline.

111

The violent night comes unawares,
it enters into my heart
breaking rhough the loose barrier
of this body that has lost its strength.
It conquers the proud beauty of my life
as my mind gives in to this attack from the dark.
When the shame of this defeat,
the insult of this tired surrender
thicken,
suddenly I see at the end of the horizon
the day's flag flying,
imprinted with lines of golden rays,
as if from some far away centre of the sky
comes the message, 'this is not true, not true'.
In the self-content light of the morning
I find at the tower of this feeble-bodied fortress
my own sorrow-conquering form.

(Arogya)
(Recovery)

Today, piercing the breast as it were of my birthday festivities
has emerged the news of a dear one's death.
My grief has burnt itself out in many a fire
to turn glowing.
The setting sun imprints the mark of blood-red glory
on the forehead of the evening; renders golden
the face of the approaching night.
So does death mark me with its burning flame.
at this west end of my life.
In its light I saw
an unbroken life where birth and death meet as one.
Sublime, it unveiled a deathlessness,
that was kept concealed under the poverty
of a niggardly fate.

(Janmadine)
(Written when the poet was eighty years old)

Standing right at the end of the courtyard
where is played the drama of creation
I gance from time to time
at the other side, beyond the dark,
where I was once immersed
in the infinite consciousness of the great Unmanifest.
This morning the words of a sage come to my mind,
'Do remove, oh sun, remove
your covering of rays,
so that I may see my true self
in your ultimate, innermost light.'
Let me not cast a shadow
–that appears as a truth –
on the path of my journey,
I, whose life breath will be absorbed
by the air at the closing of my days,
whose body will end in ashes.
In the playfield of this earth.
I have, at various moments,
tasted immortality through my joys and my sorrows,
seen the infinite on the screen of the finite,
understood that the final significance of my life
has always been there,
where reigns the beauty of the Supreme,
where plays music that is ineffable.
Now, when the doors of my playroom will soon be opened,
I shall leave my obeisance
at the earth's shrine,
leave there those offerings of my life
the value of which extends beyond death.

(Janmadine)
(Written when the poet was eighty years old)

The heat of the sun is quite severe
this lonely mid-afternoon.
I look at the empty bed-stead
for consolation – not a trace.
Its desolate bosom
speaks, as if a language of despair
Yet, its message of emptiness is not without compassion,
something that I do not quite understand.
Like a dog, masterless, who looks
with sad eyes,
to express the loss of its inconsolable mind,
not knowing what has happened and why,
but seeking night and day, pointlessly around.
The message of the bed-stead
is yet more pathetic, even more distressed.
The dumb pain of that emptiness
fills the room
with the absence of my beloved.

(Seshlekha)

Deceiver, you have scattered
nets of beguilement
throughout your creation.
With your efficient hands have set a trap
of false assurance
in a life of innocence;
and greatness is marked out
with this stratagem.
The hidden night is not for him, the great.
The path which your stars show him
is the path of his own heart.
It is transparent
and he makes this path
shine for ever
through the ease of his own faith.
However complex from outside,
he is straightforward at heart:
therein lies his pride,
harassed though he may look to others.
He finds the truth
in the depth of his own heart,
washed in its own light,
there is nothing for him to be cheated about.
Only he can collect for his own storehouse
the ultimate prize.
Only he, who can bear your deception
with impunity,
gets from your hands
the right to indestructible peace.

(Seshlekha)

116

Today I feel lost
amidst my birthday celebrations.
I wish for those friends,
through the touch of whose hands
I could take with me
this life's supreme grace,
received through the flavour of pleasing communion –
the best that this earth offers –
take with me man's final blessings.
Today my bag holds nothing,
I have emptied it,
given away whatever I had to give.
If I receive something in return –
some affection, some forgiveness –
I shall have that with me
as I take the ferry to the other side
to join in the ultimate celebration,
beyond language.

(Seshlekha)

The sun
on its very first day
struck by newly emerged existence
asked,
'who are you?'
No answer was found.
Years passed by.
The last sun of the day
asked once again,
standing on the shore of the western sea
amidst the silence of the evening
the final question –
who are you?
No response was found.

(Seshlekha)